Writing Fiction Workbook

Written and edited by Lisa Selvidge with additional material supplied by Ashley Stokes and Ian Nettleton

About the authors

D1329310

Lisa Selvidge completed a BA in Russian Language & Literature at the University of London, with Portuguese as a subsidiary. After travelling and teaching English as a Foreign Language for several years in Japan and Russia, she went on to take an MA in Creative Writing (Prose Fiction) at the University of East Anglia in the UK. She subsequently taught at the Norwich School of Art & Design for five years and then at the University of East Anglia where, in 2001, she became the Academic Director for Creative Writing in the Centre for Continuing Education. She also contributed to the BBC's *Get Writing* website.

In 2004 she moved to Portugal where she is currently living and writing for most of the year. She still teaches online prose fiction courses as well as doing freelance work and running workshops in the Algarve. For more information visit www.lisaselvidge.com

Ashley Stokes was born in 1970 in Carshalton, Surrey and was educated at St. Anne's College, Oxford and the University of East Anglia (where he took an MA in Creative Writing). He now teaches creative writing at UEA in the Centre for Continuing Education and the School of Literature and Creative Writing as well as being an associate lecturer in creative writing for the Open University and the Norwich School of Art and Design, where he teaches classes in Life Writing, Genre Fiction, Screenwriting and acts as prose tutor on the MA in Writing the Visual. His stories have appeared in This is, Pretext, EM, Hard and Other Stories: Ashley Stokes (UEA <Texts>), Take 20 (UEA), Signals 3 (London Magazines Editions), Spiked, *England Calling* (Weidenfeld and Nicolson, 2001), *Bonfire Birdsuit* and *The Creative Writing Coursebook* (Macmillan, 2001). He has written book reviews for The Guardian, the TLS, the Daily Telegraph, The Big Issue and The Good Book Guide. He won a 2002 Bridport Short Story Prize for 'The Suspicion of Bones'. He's currently writing a novel.

Ian Nettleton has a BA and MA in English Literature, and a Doctorate in Creative and Critical Writing from the University of East Anglia, where he has taught creative writing and journalism since the year 2000. He also teaches screenwriting at a cinema in Norwich and is an associate lecturer in creative writing for the Open University. He has taught at Goldsmiths College, London and has worked for a BBC digital channel, writing and presenting short synopses of works of fiction, and appeared on Radio 4's Open Book. He has a novelette appearing in *Angles*, an anthology of science fiction stories which was published in 2006 by Elastic Press, and has co-written an independent short film. He is currently working on a novel set in Australia.

Further acknowledgements:

Many thanks also to Sarah Law, Anna Garry, Sarah Bower, Christine Madsen, Helen Ivory, Caroline Gilfillan, Virginia Gay, Laura Fish, Sue Burge, Helen Cross, Nigel Curson, John Nicholson, Erica Towner, Adam Longcroft and other tutors and students from the Continuing Education creative writing team at the University of East Anglia and the Norwich School of Art & Design.

For more information on the UEA online creative writing courses, visit www.uea.ac.uk/contedu

Published by Lulu (www.lulu.com)
Non-fiction
ISBN: 978-1-84728-250-7

3. Practise fictionalising. Write a short description of yourself as someone you'd like to be - in other words, tell fibs.

4. Read through some newspapers/magazines. Cut out two or three potential stories.

5. Jot down a further two or three other potential stories from dreams, local gossip and/or family stories.

2. What is a short story?

Thinking about stories

Today, more than ever, our lives revolve around stories. Not only do we read newspapers, magazines, we listen to the radio, we watch TV/DVDs, we go to the cinema and theatre and we read anthologies of short stories and novels. But, even before the written form and the mass media age, stories have always been central to people's lives. They have been passed down through generations, not only orally but also in paintings, dance and song. In the past, as well as today, they are used to communicate, inform and entertain. From religious texts to 21st century media and art, we have always tried to make sense of the world and our lives through stories.

While this workbook focuses on prose fiction, it is worth giving a thought to different types of creative writing. For example, the novel, the memoir, travel writing, poetry, some forms of journalism, the vignette, the script (radio, TV and film), biography.

1. Take a few minutes to think about which you like and why?

Fiction differs from many of the other genres simply because it is made up. Within prose fiction we include novels, novellas and short stories but, even here, there are crossovers with other forms - some stories are quite heavily autobiographical and some memoirs are perhaps more fictional than intended. There is often a thin line between fact and fiction and when writing fiction all writers draw on their own experiences, memories and feelings to some degree. However, it is important to recognise that fiction has its own truth whereas autobiographical writing strives to be true.

What is a short story?

1. What is a short story? How does it differ from the novel? Jot down some definitions. A short story is…

2. Use the internet to search for definitions of a short story. Choose one that you think is particularly pertinent.

3. Have a look at the *Definitions of a short story* in the **Appendix**. Which one(s) do you agree with?

4. When you have finished have a look at the *Similarities and differences between novels and short stories* in the **Appendix**.

> **Tip** - **There was an interesting article by William Boyd called 'Brief Encounters' published in the Guardian Review. In it he outlines seven different types of short stories and comments on the changes in the short story market and the recent increase in its popularity. Some of the 'categories' overlap but it is interesting reading. It is useful to help you think about the kind of stories you like – and why.**
>
> **http://books.guardian.co.uk/departments/generalfiction/story/0 (Or you may have to search for author/title.)**

How short can a short story be?

1. Read the first three tales from Lynne Tillman's series **'Tales of New York'**. There are, in all, fourteen little tales, which have a cumulative effect. Nevertheless, would you consider these to be short stories? Why? How do they all begin? What happens? How do they end?

'Little Tales of New York' by Lynne Tillman, *The Time Out Book of New York Short Stories*, ed Nicholas Royle (Penguin, 1997)

1.

There was a man who loved his dog. The dog was as loyal as the day was long. But the man had a hard life and the only good thing in it was his dog. So he threw himself off the Queensboro Bridge, into the East River. He held his dog in his arms. The dog was discovered in the river tugging at the man's body. He was trying to carry his master to shore. But the man was dead, and the dog was placed in a shelter.

2.

There was a discontented woman who discovered at sixteen that she was adopted. She was relieved, because she had always been dissatisfied with her parents. The woman spent 20 years searching for her birth mother. Finally she found her, and they were reunited on Staten Island. But the woman was disappointed in her birth mother, who died shortly afterward. And for the rest of her life she regretted having looked for her.

3.

There were two teenaged brothers who loved snakes. They kept a 13 foot Burmese Python in the Bronx project where they lived. They hoped to make a career out of caring for reptiles. But one day, when one of the brothers was about to feed the snake a live chicken, the python mistook the brother for prey. The brother was found lying down in a pool of his own blood in the hallway of the apartment building. The snake was still coiled around his midriff and back. Their mother had asked her sons to get rid of the python, but she recognised her son's passion for reptiles. 'He loved animals,' she said. 'He went to the zoo all the time.'

2. Try writing your own little tale of your town/village/city.
There was a...

3. Lynne Tillman's tales are stripped down to the bone yet they still contain the basic essence of a story. They have characters, a beginning, middle and end, and have the power to move the reader. Now read **'Eclipsed'** by Robert Schuster. How does it differ from Lynne Tillman's tales? For comment see the **Appendix.**

Micro Fiction, **edited by Jerome Stern (Norton, 1996)**

Eclipsed
Robert Shuster

Anxious not to miss the coming darkness, Gavin woke early and watched Dad construct the viewers from boxes. Behind his pile of aluminium foil, cardboard, and glue, Dad said: "You see, when the moon passes in front of the sun, like this" - he held up his hairy fists before his eyes - "my head, the earth, gets dark."

The hour approached. Standing expectantly on the front lawn, their backs to the sun, they donned their viewers. Muffled by cardboard, Dad's voice sounded distant: "See the black dot? That's the moon."

Gavin watched the white and black dot converge, his moist fingers pressed against the box. Twice he glanced through the neck hole to see if his body was wilting, or his feet sinking. He imagined the darkness - moon darkness - coating his hands.

"There," came the distant voice. "Completely covered. Hell, the next time this happens, I'll be dead."

Gavin shook off the viewer. The summer grass was brown, the sky purple. He looked at the forbidden sight - the covered sun, the patched yellow eye - and tried, quickly, to imagine his father dead and himself a man, to imagine years passing as the earth spun a thousand times. Dad, darkened, stood still, his square cardboard head bent to the ground, a space creature. Gavin jammed the box on his head. He wanted the sun.

What kind of stories do you like?

1. We tend to (and, indeed, we should) write what we most like to read. When you are back home, have a look through your bookshelves and see what books you have most of. Do you enjoy genre fiction (crime, romance, historical, science fiction, fantasy or children's fiction)? Or perhaps you read strictly literary fiction? Jot down your preferences and then consider why you like them. Refer back to your potential stories – do they reflect your taste?

2. Without thinking about this exercise too much, choose a character type (a doctor, a builder, a teacher, a policeman, a deep sea diver, an astronaut, a microbiologist, an aerialist…) and a place (Mars, central London, an underground station, a cruise ship, a museum, a park, a morgue…) Now imagine the character is standing in the setting and sees something very strange. What is it? How does the character react? What happens next? Write for 20 minutes – you may need to use another notebook here. What kind of genre have you written?

Reading a short story (1)

1. Choose any short story (for example, choose one from www.short-stories.co.uk) and consider the following points: Setting, characters, events, themes, plot, conflict (refer again to the *Similarities and differences between novels and short stories*).

3. Location, location, location

Locations are not only sought after by property developers and TV producers, but also by writers. Many writers are inspired by other countries, cities, exotic and strange landscapes.

PD James writes, 'Usually my creative imagination is sparked off by the setting rather than by the method of murder or by any of the characters. I have a strong reaction to place and may visit a lonely stretch of coast, a sinister old house or a community of people and feel strongly that I wish to set a novel there.'
(quoted from www.randomhouse.com/features/pdjames/faq.html)

But even mundane settings should be collected, wherever possible, and stored up in a location bank. You never know when you may use them. A part of your story (or all of it) may be set in a school, in an office, in a hospital, by the sea, on a mountainside, on a train, in a restaurant, in Russia, in your street, your town, a place you visited on holiday. The list is endless. At the time of visiting somewhere you may think that you'll never forget the place but ten years later, when you need it, it has become hazy. Writing about locations is also a good way to begin writing and to practise writing description.

Using the senses – the 3 Ss and 2 Ts

Sight, sound, smell, touch and taste are the five senses that help to create a believable setting.

1. Next time you're out, take your notebook and jot down as many details as you can about three different locations.

For example:

1. **A train/bus station, airport/port**
2. **Inner city street**
3. **A seaside resort**
4. **A building (inside and out)**

Use the following questions as guidelines:

Visual detail

What kind of buildings/landscape surround you?

What are the street names/shops?

What kind of phone boxes are there? Or beach huts?

What types of cars?

What kind of litter?

What is written on the van of an ice-cream seller?

What are people wearing?

What kind of life is there around you?

What is the writing on the wall?

Atmospheric detail

What is the weather like?

What time of year is it?

What time of day?

What kind of light is there?

What sort of feel is there to the place?

What can you smell?

What can you touch?

What can you hear?

What can you taste?

What makes a setting believable?

When writing *Lord of the Rings*, Tolkien had a map, so he knew where his characters were going. His world was real to him. More than that, it was probably based on his own memories of the England he knew. Philip K. Dick's stories are science fiction stories – for example, *Minority Report* and *Blade Runner* (from the novel, *Do Androids Dream of Electric Sheep*) – but what makes them believable? They are partly based on the world he knew. Daphne du Maurier's short story, *The Birds*, tells of an England where birds have destroyed civilisation, but it was set on the south coast of England – a landscape she knew.

1. In your memory, revisit a place you know well. Make a list of the things you remember. If you can, go back to that place and observe. How do the two descriptions compare?

2. Look at the following excerpt from a story by Graham Greene called 'Across the Bridge' (Graham Greene, *Collected Short Stories*, Penguin, 1986).

> 'They say he's worth a million,' Lucia said. He sat there in the little hot damp Mexican square, a dog at his feet, with an air of immense and forlorn patience. The dog attracted your attention at once; for it was very nearly an English setter, only something had gone wrong with the tail and the feathering. Palms wilted over his head, it was all shade and stuffiness round the bandstand, radios talked loudly in Spanish from the little wooden sheds where they changed your pesos into dollars at a loss. I could tell he didn't understand a word from the way he read his newspaper – as I did myself picking out the words which were like English ones. 'He's been here a month,' Lucia said, 'they turned him out of Guatemala and Honduras.'

What makes you believe in the place? Look at the small selective details that make the world of the story believable.

Across the Bridge is set in Mexico, and Greene only visited the place for a short while as a reporter. The above description sketches the Mexican town, while a lot of detail is left out. It is selective. It also says something about the main character, who is wanted by the police. He is trapped in a world of boredom. As writers we must be selective about what details of the world we put into our story. Some writers only sketch their settings, preferring to focus on the characters and action, others use elaborate backgrounds and atmosphere as a way of illuminating character and action. Whichever style we prefer, we still need to be selective about what we use and remember that it is the detail that makes writing distinctive and settings realistic.

4. Time and research

Settings do not only include location, but also time. The world is constantly changing and it is important for stories to be firmly anchored in an era. It may be one day in 1980 or it may be loosely set in 'the present'. Or it could be set in the future (which, of course, would rely on the imagination). Details such as the political background, topical issues of the day, programmes on TV, brand names, advertising, fashions, current sayings, music, types of transport... all help to show when your story is set.

As Faulkner said, writers need experience, observation and imagination, but they also need to research - and, indeed, research can supply the lack of the others. You may need to research the type of job your character does, the setting, illnesses your characters' may suffer from, different ways of murdering, ways of travelling from London to Paris, the price of petrol in 1974... The list is endless.

The internet and the library are, of course, invaluable for doing research. You can also combine research and observation by visiting places and talking to people. For example, if your character is a fire fighter, go down to the local fire station and ask if you can arrange to speak to someone. Public service workers (fire, police, local politicians) are usually very happy to talk to you about their work – providing they have the time. There are also many documentaries and films which can be useful.

Clearly, historical fiction needs more research. Much more. Make sure you read lots of historical fiction and watch films around the era you wish to write. You need to get your facts right to make the story convincing. Again, as Faulkner says, it also helps to have some experience of the world you are writing about. While you can not travel backwards in time, you can try to recreate some of the events/settings. For example, if your character sets sail in a caravel, try to sail in one yourself - even if it is just a tourist attraction.

When writing in the future, more imagination than research is needed. But, in order to imagine a convincing world, you need to have a fairly good grasp of technology and how things could be.

Assignment: From fact to fiction

We have discussed the differences between fact and fiction, and how writers blend their own experience with observation, imagination and research. The following assignment is to get you thinking about the process of fictionalisation.

Choose an age between seven and ten. Think about where you lived, where you went to school, what your parents or guardians did. Then think of something that happened: a fight at school, a telling-off from a teacher, a meeting with a stranger, perhaps you were on holiday, somewhere you shouldn't have been… Research the background detail on the internet. What political events were going on that year? What music was in the charts? What did you see/hear/smell?

Write up your adventure in the first person (i.e. 'I') – two pages approximately.

Read again Robert Shuster's 'Eclipsed'. Then rewrite your story – only this time, fictionalise it. To begin with, change the character. Write 'he' or 'she' instead of 'I'. If you are male, write 'she' and vice versa. You might also want to change the ending. What would have happened if…? Or, perhaps, the era. Keep your fictionalised story under 1,000 words.

PART 2 - MIDDLES

The Story

The aim here is to guide you through the mechanics of writing a story. The 3 major steps include how to structure, how to create three dimensional characters, and how to narrate. Hopefully, by now you have an idea that you want to develop - perhaps refer back to *Sources for stories,* or maybe you will be inspired by an exercise in this section.

1. What's the plot?

'So the plot is the source and (as it were) the soul of tragedy; character is second.' Aristotle, *Poetics*, Penguin, 1966

Before disagreeing, try the following warm up.

Word warm up

1. Take a dictionary, choose 3 words at random and write a paragraph incorporating all three words.

Character versus plot

There has been much debate within creative writing groups and academia about the competing importance of plot and character. *Aristotle* (for more information see the **Appendix**) argued that plot is more important than character. He reasoned that the aim of tragedy is to evoke fear and pity. Fear and pity are responses to success and failure, and success and failure depend on action, therefore plot is more important than character ...

Joining the debate

1. Which do you think is more important? Jot down some examples of stories that are more action based and some which are more character based. Are characters or the plots more memorable? Is there a pattern emerging?

Of course, it depends on the genre and the fact is character and plot work together in a symbiotic relationship. One cannot exist without the other. An event forces the character to act in a particular way and, in doing so, reveals the true character. As Henry James said,

'What is character but the determination of incident? What is incident but the illustration of character?' Henry James, 'The Art of Fiction', collected in *Partial Portraits*, (first published in 1888).

Stories are about change, hence the give-away titles of early collections of tales, like Ovid's *The Metamorphoses*. There should be a moment of change in a story, either of overcoming an obstacle or achieving a moment of realisation. In developing characters you are essentially finding ways in which they change through the pressure of events or reflection. Without a sense of change, a story is trivial.

Beginnings, middles & ends

Aristotle is more famously known for saying that all stories must have a *beginning, middle and end* (see **Appendix**) – as, in fact, this workbook has. It is a simplistic breakdown of the structure of the story, but an accurate one.

John Galsworthy in *Selected Essays and Addresses* (Heinemann, 1932) likens Chekhov's stories to tortoises; they were all middle he thought. This is important for short stories which do not have the space for lengthy descriptions at the beginning outlining the initial situation. They also rarely tie things up at the end. Short stories are more concerned with the conflict in the middle and, as a result, often begin *in medias res* (in the middle of things).

GEORGE FRANJU: Movies should have a beginning, a middle and an end.
JEAN-LUC GODARD: Certainly. But not necessarily in that order.
(in Time 14 September 1981)

Although this quote refers to films, the same applies to all stories. This is where it might be useful to think about the difference between story and plot.

Story/plot

There is often confusion between the terms 'story' and 'plot'. We tend to use the two words interchangeably but there is a difference. A story is a fictional account of an event or series of events, whereas a plot refers to the actual *sequence* or *arrangement* of events. Perhaps think then of a story as the overall picture and the plot as the detail.

The difference can be illustrated in a simple crime/detective story.

1. Two men plan to rob a bank.
2. The crime is committed and the robbers escape by car.
3. The police arrive on the scene and start their investigations.
4. The two robbers argue about the money.

5. One man shoots the other, drops the gun and goes to the airport, taking all the money with him.
6. The police trace the car and discover the man who has been shot, but find that he is still alive.
7. The dying man tells the police his partner's name.
8. The police apprehend the man at the airport.

1-8 make up the story. The particular arrangement of 1-8 refers to the plot. Detective fiction often starts with a murder so the writer may choose another plot and start with 4, 5, or 6 and reveal 1, 2 and 3 as the story progresses.

> 1. In order to practise the arrangement of plots, take a simple newspaper story and break it down into events. Then write each event on a separate strip of paper and mix them up and find a different way of plotting the story by rearranging events.

The 3 Cs

> 1. Perhaps more important when thinking about story structure is to remember the 3 Cs - **Characters**, **Conflict** and **Crisis.** Conflict is particularly important as it is the link between character and plot. Without conflict there is no story.
>
> What kinds of conflicts are there? Which form is particularly suitable to prose fiction? (See **Appendix** for suggestions).

Nearly all stories will contain the 3 Cs. They will also have a setting, a trigger, a quest (however small), a critical moment - if not a fully fledged crisis - leading to a climax and usually some kind of resolution, surprise or closure. The story structure looks something like this:

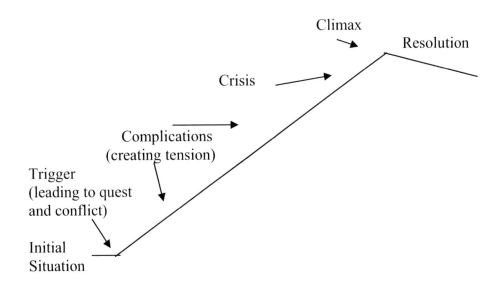

Climax

Resolution

Crisis

Complications
(creating tension)

Trigger
(leading to quest
and conflict)

Initial
Situation

Thinking about structure

1. Read through any story. Identify the characters, the conflict, the trigger (or inciting incident) the quest, the setting, the crisis (and/or climax).

2. Outline a story. For example, a brother and a sister (**characters**) go to the seaside (**setting**) for the day. They have saved up money to go and have been looking forward to it - in particular, they want to go to the Sea World (**quest**). When they get there, the sister is tempted to spend their money in the arcades. Her brother tries to stop her (**conflict**). She loses all their money (**crisis**). They do not have any money to get home. The brother storms off, leaving her alone (**climax**). She goes to the beach and sits down on the sand. Something silver catches her eye…(**resolution**).

3. Get a friend to give you the name of a character and a setting (time and place). From these elements create skeletal plots (no more than four sentences) which have an initial situation, trigger, crisis and resolution. Don't write the actual story.

Extreme structure – Propp & fairytales

1. A Russian formulist, **Vladimir Propp**, spent his life collating and analysing the structure of Russian folk tales. He published his influential *Morphology of the Folktale* in 1928 (first translated in 1958). His structural analysis may seem extreme but it is a useful way of breaking down stories. Try plotting a fairytale like 'Little Red Riding Hood' onto the functions (see the **Appendix**). Does it work? Consider a modern-day fairytale like *Star Wars*. Compare the characters in the film to Propp's character types - hero, villain, helper, dispatcher, donor, Princess (or sought for person), false hero.

2. Use Propp's functions to write your own tale.

Time, place & action

Aristotle is also credited for the three dramatic unities of time, place and action, but this is not strictly true. He was only ever really concerned with the unity of action. However, as most stories are connected in time, place and action, it is a useful way of discussing the 'who' 'what', 'when' 'where' and 'why' of a story.

We have now considered the difference between plot and story and discussed how short a short story can be in Part 1 but we have not fully examined what actually makes a story 'a story' (or narrative) - other than it being a complete picture. As we have mentioned, when we talk about plot, we are usually referring to the events that happen. However, events on their own are not enough in themselves to make a story. Consider the following:

A woman lies awake. She paces up and down. The glass breaks. The doorbell rings.

As a piece of writing, there is nothing wrong with this 'stream of consciousness' style, but it would be hard to call it a 'story'. It is not like Lynne Tillman's short tales, for example. Such isolated events produce a fragmented picture from which we can vaguely sense that something is wrong. We have a character, a woman, but the narrative, as it stands, is too disconnected for us to fully understand - there are too many gaps to fill in. This is because there are no causal, temporal or spacial connections between events. We know *what* happens, but we do not know *why* they happen or *when* or *where* these events happen. However, if we connect up the actions - albeit roughly - we have a complete story.

A woman lies awake at night in her bedsit in Hammersmith. Her boyfriend has stormed out after a row at dinner and threatened not to return. In the early hours of the morning, she paces up and down the bedroom, crying. She picks up a glass from the bedside table and throws it at the wall. The glass breaks and the jagged edges glisten on the carpet. She sits down on the bed wondering where he is. The doorbell rings. She wipes her face and goes to answer it. He is holding a bunch of flowers.

We now know why the woman can not sleep, why she walks around the room, why the glass breaks and why the doorbell rings. All the events are connected in causality. This is the unity of action. We also know where and when these events happen. These connections help to complete the whole picture. Substitute 'bunch of flowers' for 'a gun' and we've raised the stakes, created tension.

Making connections

Connect one of these series of sentences (or make your own up) in time, place and action.

i) A door shuts. A woman laughs. Snow is falling. A dog barks. The woman walks in the snow.

ii) A bell tolls from a temple. A girl runs through the streets. The smell of chestnuts fills the air. A plate is thrown out of a window.

iii) A man cries. Blood trickles down the wall. The sound of a helicopter. A toilet flushes.

iv) A ship sails across the sea. A mother shouts at her child. A fish gasps for breath. A bar of soap sinks into the water.

Theme

Think also of the theme: what is the story really about? Is it about disappointment? Growing up? Loss? Jealousy? But a theme should never be stated.

Assignment: Plotting the story

For this assignment, aim to work on an outline for a skeletal story structure.

Write in note form the setting (time and place) and the character(s), the initial situation, the trigger - leading to quest and conflict - the complications and the crisis/climax. Consider: what is the story really about?

You can, of course, simply use the assignment as an exercise on structure but, if you can, try to plot a story that you would like to develop throughout the rest of the workbook.

> **Tip - Not all writers plan and structure their stories, but most do. It is not quite so important for shorter stories, but crucial for longer fiction. Even if you choose not to use the outlines, practising structure is a useful exercise.**

2. Who is she, really?

'If you let your characters live, and get out of their way, then you have a chance of creating something individual.' Ray Bradbury
(quoted from www.raybradbury.com/articles_bestselling.html interviewed by Mark Levy reprinted from Bookselling this Week, Feb.1997)

Before we find out who she really is, or what she really wants, try the following:

Word warm up

1. Think of an animal. Describe yourself as that animal without actually mentioning what you are. How old are you? What are you made of? What shape are you? What colour are you? What do you do? Where do you live? What do you like about life? What makes you laugh? What makes you cry? What is your greatest fear? What is your idea of happiness? What will become of you? Write for 15 minutes.

Looks should be deceptive

In the previous section we debated the importance of character and plot, and we concluded that one very much depends on the other. But, as we also mentioned, different genres place greater emphasis on either story/plot or characterisation. We could say that an adventure/action story, for example, relies heavily on an external physical plot, whereas a psychological thriller focuses more on the internal cognitive workings of character.

You need to have a clear idea, then, of readership and genre. What sort of story are you writing? What are the expectations of the readers who consume this genre? If you don't know, then read around a bit. Given the nature of the story, does it need a definite resolution, as most romances and crime stories have, or will a more open ending suffice? How much does the character have to change for the story to satisfy?

Our knowledge of such genre expectations, daily emphasised by mainstream films and television, creates a danger of depicting stereotypes. One thing you should try to avoid is stereotypes. An interesting character should be not quite what he or she seems.

This is why it is worth doing exercises on creating characters. Think of your characters as real people. What motivates them? What do they want? What are they afraid of? How would they react to a specific situation? Learn as much as you can about your characters. Not all this information needs to be present in a story. Most of it is for you as author only. And remember, to look and to listen to other people. This way you will learn how to create memorable three dimensional characters.

Memorable characters

1. Jot down which characters you remember from books and films.

2. What makes a character memorable?

3. What do you think is the difference between characterisation and true character? When you have finished, look up **Characterisation** in the **Appendix.**

4. Think of some ways in which you could look for interesting characters? When you have finished go to **Sources for Characters** in the **Appendix.**

4. Sit in a cafe or marketplace and write a description of some of the people around you - without making it too obvious! What interests you about the way people act, dress or behave? Get into the habit of describing body language. How do people sit in relation to one another in different situations? How do they walk? What is it about a newly encountered person that tells you what their intentions are?

Reading a short story (2)

1. Read another short story and focus on the character(s). How is the main character introduced? What does she want? What are her contradictions? What motivates her? How are the characters physically described?

(As a revision exercise, consider also the structure of the story. What is the initial situation? The trigger? Quest? Conflict? Complications? Crisis? What is the theme?)

Developing your own characters

1. You might start by writing a chronology of your main character. Think about where they were born, what environment they grew up in, where they went to school, first loves, first jobs etc. Make this as detailed as possible, adding as much anecdotal and descriptive material as possible. You want a clear idea of where a person has come from if you are to have an understanding of where they are going. What you are looking for here are turning points, moments where the world changed irreversibly, where insight and understanding was found, where the character experienced realisation or was forced to act in a new way. When did he or she first realise that the world is entirely different to what he or she had assumed? Moments of change for a character are the stuff of fiction. Be inventive here. Don't settle for the first thing that comes into your head. Up the stakes with key events. Make them stand out. Make them complicated. Make sure that there are consequences.

2. Now fill out the *Character Creation* form in the **Appendix**.

3. Write your character's obituary (bearing in mind the author of the obituary and their relationship to the character).

5. Make a list of what all the main character's family and friends think of them.

6. Write a section in which you convey your character's essential qualities by listing what they carry in their pockets, handbag, or briefcase.

How do your characters interact with each other and the story?

What a character wants is a good rule of thumb for what they are going to do in terms of action and interaction. A character wants something: a date, the answers, the money… but they can't have it, so they take risks until they eventually win or lose. A character who behaves like this would be a protagonist. They act. They are defined by their actions and what they are prepared to risk. They would be the centre of the story, maybe the narrator. The protagonist has most at stake in the story, most to lose, and most to gain. The obstacle, or the person in their way, is the antagonist. Of course, if you write from the point of view of the antagonist, you are changing the story. Different types of stories have different types of protagonists/antagonists. Genre fiction such as romances and crime novels depend upon risk taking and obstacles to generate forward drive and tension and use more archetypal heroes and villains. These stories frequently depend upon a 'what' factor. What happens next? In stories such as these, the character needs to be up to the task but likely to be tested by it.

Other types of stories use more circumspect characters. Conflict may be less external, more internal, the drama more low-key but nonetheless dramatic. Stories that are a slice of life or concerning events such as weddings and funerals, vignettes which serve to delineate a personality, these stories rely less on the neat plot curves of popular fiction and more on a sense of 'why?' and 'how?' Often a question is asked at the outset that is explored throughout the narrative.

A character in a minimally plotted story needs more depth and dimensions than an archetypal protagonist. They are more likely to exist to show and explain than they are to act and achieve. A whole person's life may be illuminated in the events of one day without the need for the bang and crash of romance and conspiracy.

Whichever type of story you are writing, the characters need to be suitably different from each other and you need to ensure there is enough tension between them. Three friends who are all nice to each other will not make a good story.

> **Tip - Make sure that if you have more than three characters in a short story they are all necessary.**

Types of characters

1. Consider the characters in your story. Are they different enough? What roles are they playing? Are they there for a reason? Can you identify the protagonist and the antagonist? Is there sufficient conflict and/or tension between the characters?

Assignment: Going for a walk with her

Take your character for a walk. Use the third person narrative voice and forbid yourself from entering her head. Write as if you are a camera following her, providing only external gestures and impressions for the reader. Ask yourself, how can I describe what she is thinking without using dialogue or comment?

3. What does he sound like?

The voice of your character(s)

Writing dialogue is part of writing a story. There are very few stories without dialogue and there are very few stories that consist only of dialogue. It is estimated that approximately one third of any story should be dialogue (although the percentage can vary greatly). How a character speaks, both in dialogue and internally, is fundamental to the story. This fictional voice will be informed by the character's background. Narrative voice also plays a part here. If a character is telling a story, from where are they telling it? What is the narrative distance? After the event? If so, how far away are we from the event? The tone of voice of an old man telling a story from his boyhood will differ from the same story told from a closer vantage point. Or is the story set very much in the present, as if we are inside the character's head as things are happening to him? This will obviously have an effect on the diction and on the extent to which you can meditate. The narrative voice always sets up a series of constraints but within these constraints you can be creative.

These we might see as external factors that influence the voice. You want to marry these with individual elements, insights and eccentricities personal to that one person. This is what we call idiolect, the way an individual speaks. Here, you need to be on top of your background work and create a voice that reflects that experience. This becomes very much how we depict a character from the inside, how we construct a point of view. At every stage, whether the character is talking to themselves or engaged in dialogue with others, you need to be feeding through all of the character's experience to date into those lines. If you can provide the reader with a fresh slant on the commonplace, if you can draw their attention to things around them that they always knew were there but hadn't yet realised it, you are halfway there to creating a voice. Or should we say voices. People do not use the same voice in all circumstances.

Beginning writers often find writing dialogue slightly daunting at first but, like everything else, it is a matter of practising. Eudora Welty writes that,

'Once you're into a story everything seems to apply – what you overhear on a city bus is exactly what your character would say on the page you're writing. Wherever you go, you meet a part of your story. I guess you tuned in for it, and the right things are sort of magnetised – if you can think of your ears as magnets.' 'The Art of Fiction' no 47 Paris Review (www.parisreview.com/media/4013_Welty.pdf)

Even if this doesn't happen, it is useful to remember Natalie Goldberg's advice that writers should 'listen well and deeply'. Listen to different people's rhythm, use of verbs and slang.

What does dialogue do?

1. What do you think dialogue should do? Make some notes.

2. Go and sit in a public space and listen into people's conversations. Try to record verbatim what people are saying? Could you use this so-called 'real dialogue' in a story? If not, why not? Go to *Functions of Dialogue* in the **Appendix** for more information.

3. Read the following dialogue taken from Carrie Worrall's *Grace*. What does it tell us about the main character Derek? How does the author show us how he feels? What kind of character is Barrow? How is the suspense built?

Extract taken from *Grace* by Carrie Worrall (Piatkus, 1998, p233)

'I had personal reasons for changing my name,' says Derek. 'I was protecting my family. There is no law against it, is there?'

Barrow's eyes twinkle with cynicism, and he blows on his cup of tea.

'I bet Mr Ridley would agree with you there,' he says. 'I'm sure he's done the same by now, and your Miss Scales.'

'You haven't traced them, then?'

'Cheeky really, they paid for flights to America via Schipol, and pre-booked the car hire all on Mrs Ridley's credit card. They're probably in Mexico by now.'

'Just like that?'

'Oh, you never know. They might not get away with it. Sometimes the past just catches up with you, doesn't it?'

Derek ignores this and sips his coffee. It tastes bitter. He knows that Rachel keeps a couple of sachets of sugar squirreled away, and crosses the room to look for them.

'Do you mind if I ask about your relationship with Mr Ridley?' asks Barrow.

Derek shrugs as he slides open the top drawer of Rachel's desk.

'Not at all, but there's nothing much to tell. We've worked together here for a couple of years, but we didn't socialise.'

'You didn't know each other in Newcastle, then?'

How does he talk?

If your character speaks another language than their mother tongue, or is from a place with a distinctive dialect, you need to think carefully about phonetically transcribing colloquial language. Each city, as well as country, has its own dialect and, while it is fun to try and capture the rhythms and sounds of that dialect, there is a danger that the language might sound clichéd or incomprehensible. There are writers who do successfully write in the vernacular (read the extract from **James Kelman** in the **Appendix**), but it is hard to do well. Instead, perhaps try to think of other ways of capturing another language/dialect. Listen to the rhythms of the language and play with word order.

1. Try making up certain phrases that make your character's dialect distinctive - but careful not to overdo it.

2. Compile a list of situations, some ordinary, like ordering a pizza, some extreme, like ordering a coffin, and construct a line of speech or observation that sums up how your character would negotiate these occasions.

3. We all know that while we are saying one thing we are often thinking something very different or contrary. Write a passage of dialogue in which the thoughts of your character occasionally break onto the page.

The act of writing dialogue

There are two types of dialogue: direct and indirect. An example of direct dialogue would be: **'Frank didn't look very well this morning,' said John**. An example of indirect dialogue would be: **John said that Frank didn't look very well this morning.**

1. Practise writing direct and indirect dialogue.

2. There are, at least, a 100 different ways of saying 'said'. Jot down some of them? What is the problem with using these verbs? For advice on how to carry dialogue go to the **Appendix**.

Note - Layout of dialogue is explained in Part 3.

Assignment: Meeting him

Now that you know what your character looks like, how he behaves and talks, it is time to introduce him. A classic way of introducing a character is to have other characters talking about him, then seeing him from afar and then, finally, meeting him. In short stories there is rarely time and space to do this in detail. A famous example is the introduction of Sally Bowles in **Christopher Isherwood's** *The Berlin Novels* (see **Appendix**). Note how there is a sense of curiosity when she arrives - late - as she has already been described as someone who perhaps is not quite what she seems. The telling detail of the green nail-varnish shows us much about her personality. Note also Fritz' use of 'eventually' instead of 'actually', 'only half of an hour' and his play with word order which helps capture his first language.

Write the introduction of your main character (500 words approx.). It may be the beginning or it may be later on in your story - it doesn't matter.

4. Whose story is it and who's telling it?

'If all but one of the instruments on a surgeon's tray had been sterilised, that exception would be a danger to the patient. It can be said that one slip of point of view by a writer can hurt a story badly, and several slips can be fatal.' Sol Stein, *Stein on Writing,* St Martin's Press, 1995

Before we look at how slips in viewpoint can be fatal, have a go at the following warm-up.

Word warm up

1. Choose two objects in your room or somewhere around you. Pretend that you are one object describing the other - without actually mentioning what either of you are. As with other writing exercises, focus on the senses.

Who? When? How?

Narrative point of view is the most complex and, at times, the most slippery topic in prose fiction. This is not helped by the fact that when we talk about point of view we could be referring to two slightly different things. Firstly, we say, for example, that the story is told from the point of view of a particular character (i.e. the killer, the babysitter, the victim and so on). The story of two sisters separated at birth and brought up in different cultures would make up two very different stories depending on *whose story (or point of view)* is being told. The story of a man running off with a lover would be a different story told from the wife's point of view or the lover's. The story of a bank robbery could be told from the point of view of the robbers or the people who are in the bank. And so on. Secondly, point of view sometimes refers to *how you tell your story* (first person, second person, third person detached, omniscient and so on).

To recap then, the first thing to decide is **whose story is it?** (Even omniscient narration will usually favour some characters more than others. Totally objective narration would probably be closer to journalism or historiography.)

> **Tip - If you feel a story isn't working and you don't know why, it may be that you are telling the wrong story. Who has the problem/quest?**

A related point, as we discussed in section 3, is the narrative distance. **From where and when is the story being told?** We suggested that the voice of an old man telling a story from his boyhood will differ from the same story told from a closer vantage point. These decisions about the narration will determine the overall shape and tone of your story, and will either contribute to its success or be its failure. The greatest story in the world, if inappropriately told, will fall flat on its face.

Deciding which narrative point of view to use

1. You have already decided on what happens in your story, you know your characters inside out, you know whose story it is, you know how the character(s) think, talk, walk. So now you have to

make the most crucial decision: how are you going to tell your story? Jot down all the different forms of narration you can think of to tell a story. Think of different tenses as well as viewpoints.

When you have finished, look up *Forms of narration* in the **Appendix**. We will consider them in more detail below.

Practising different narrative forms

In contemporary writing you may do anything you like with point of view - as long as it works. There are pros and cons for the various viewpoints but the only rule is to be consistent. We would advise against omniscience, unless you are very sure that it is the only way to tell your story.

> **Note - In the examples cited below, we have referred to longer works of fiction which are more likely to be known.**

First person

To beginning writers, this often seems like an easy option. However, to write well in the first person requires much skill. You really have to know your character. There are also many different kinds of first person narratives.

Firstly, there is the **storyteller** or raconteur. This is one of the oldest forms of narration, a direct descendant of oral story telling, and, possibly, the least used in contemporary fiction. An updated version would be a narrator who tells a story to an assembled group of interested people in a pub or round a campfire. The narrator would be a minor character - perhaps even relating a story he had heard - who would be fairly neutral while telling the story. The story would be narrated in the past tense and the protagonist would be someone else. A classic modern example is the narrator in Conrad's *Heart of Darkness*. He is aboard the *Nellie* with several other crew members, including Marlow. The narrator in such tales would usually be **a reliable narrator.** This means that we have no reason to question the veracity of the narrative.

The storyteller, modern or not, may be an **intrusive narrator/author** (i.e. an author who keeps interrupting the narratives with various asides to the reader - for example, in George Elliot's novels.). In more contemporary works the intrusion is usually more self-conscious, such as in *Howard's End* by E.M. Forster. An earlier example is the narrator of Henry Fielding's *Tom Jones* (1749). (Compare also the omniscient narrator in the section on ***Third person*** below).

It is more common in contemporary fiction to have the main character as narrator, meaning that the character narrates their own story. Some first person novels almost span the narrator's entire life and, indeed, it is what the novel does well. They are written from a later point in life and are therefore able to be retrospective. An early example is Daniel Defoe's *Moll Flanders*. A more recent example is William Boyd's *Any Human Heart* (written in the form of several journals with the character occasionally commenting on them at a later date). However, most first person novels, and particularly short stories, will focus on a part of a character's life.

If the character's account does not seem to hold together seamlessly, it may be because he or she is **an unreliable narrator**. The term does not necessarily mean that the narrator is a habitual liar (although that could be the case), it may be that the narrator is naïve or ill informed. A classic example is Huck in Mark Twain's *Adventures of Huckleberry Fin* (1884) in which the 14-year-old narrator does not fully understand the significance of the events he is relating and commenting on. A more contemporary example is Humbert Humbert in Nabokov's ***Lolita*** and Saleem Sinai in Salman Rushdie's *Midnight's Children* - although neither of these narrators is naïve or ill informed.

Mark Twain's *Adventures of Huckleberry Fin* is also an early example of teenage **skaz**. This term comes from the Russian verb skazat' (to say) and refers to young narrators who narrate their story in a colloquial voice fairly soon after the events. J.D. Salinger's *The Catcher in the Rye* is the classic twentieth century example. Here, the conversational narrative appears to be spontaneous but it is, in actual fact, a carefully constructed narrative.

There are also **epistolary novels**. These are novels written in the form of a series of letters or journals. It was a form of narrative often use in the 18th century. A classic example is Richardson's *Pamela* (1740-1) and *Clarissa* (1747-8). Modern novels include John Barth's *Letters* or the already mentioned William Boyd's *Any Human Heart*. A contemporary variation would be a novel composed of emails. Diary novels are also very popular: Helen Fielding's *Bridget Jones's diary* is an excellent contemporary example. Like teenage skaz, novels composed of diary entries/blogs and letters are slightly different in that the main character and narrator must be telling the story, more or less, from the present. It need not use the present tense - although it may do - but the narrator needs to be rooted in the story as it happens and is therefore unable to be retrospective – unless the character/author masquerades as 'editor'.

---

1. Read through the extract of ***Lolita***. Why do you think Humbert Humbert is an unreliable narrator?

Extract from Lolita by Vladimir Nabokov, Penguin, 1980 (first published in 1959), p. 9

1.

LOLITA, light of my life, fire of my loins. My sin, my soul. Lo-lee-ta: the tip of the tongue making a trip of three steps down the palate to tap, at three, on the teeth. Lo. Lee. Ta.

She was Lo, plain Lo, in the morning, standing four feet ten in one sock. She was Lola in slacks. She was Dolly at school. She was Dolores on the dotted line. But in my arms she was always Lolita.

Did she have a precursor? She did, indeed she did. In point of fact, there might have been no Lolita at all had I not loved, one summer, a certain initial girl-child. In a princedom by the sea. Oh when? About as many years before Lolita was born as my age was that summer. You can always count on a murderer for a fancy prose style.

Ladies and gentlemen of the jury, exhibit number one is what the seraphs, the misinformed, simple noble-winged seraphs, envied. Look at this tangle of thorns.

---

2. Read through the following extract from **Bridget Jones's diary**. Where is the narrator situated? How does she recount past events?

Extract from Bridget Jones's diary by Helen Fielding, Picador, 1996 (pp 10-11)

11.45 p.m. Ugh. First day of New Year has been day of horror. Cannot quite believe I am once again starting the year in a single bed in my parents' house. It is too humiliating at my age. I wonder if they'll smell it if I have a fag out of the window. Having skulked at home all day, hoping hangover would clear, I eventually gave up and set off for the Turkey Curry Buffet far too late. When I got to the Alconburys' and rang their entire-tune-of-town-hall-clock-style doorbell I was still in a strange world of my own - nauseous, vile-headed, acidic. I was also suffering from road-rage residue after inadvertently getting on to the M6 instead of the M1 and having to drive halfway to Birmingham before I could find anywhere to turn round. I was so furious I kept jamming my foot down to the floor on the accelerator pedal to give vent to my feelings, which is very dangerous. I watched resignedly as Una Alconbury's form - intriguingly deformed through the ripply glass door - bore down on me in a fuchsia two-piece.

'Bridget! We'd almost given you up for lost! Happy New Year! Just about to start without you.'

She seemed to manage to kiss me, get my coat off, hang it over the banister, wipe her lipstick of my cheek and make me feel incredibly guilty all in one movement, while I leaned against the ornament shelf for support.

'Sorry. I got lost.'

'Lost? Durr! What are we going to do with you? Come on in!'

She led me through the frosted-glass doors into the lounge, shouting, 'She got lost, everyone!'

'Bridget! Happy New Year!' said Geoffrey Alconbury, clad in a yellow diamond-patterned sweater. He did a jokey Bruce Forsyth step then gave me the sort of hug which Boots would send straight to the police station.

'Hahumph,' he said, going red in the face and pulling his trousers up by the waistband. 'Which junction did you come off at?'

'Junction nineteen, but there was a diversion...'

'Junction nineteen! Una, she came off at Junction nineteen! You've added an hour to your journey before you even started. Come on, let's get you a drink. How's your love-life, anyway?'

Oh *God.* Why can't married people understand that this is no longer a polite question to ask? We wouldn't rush up to *them* and roar, 'How's your marriage going? Still having sex?' Everyone knows that dating in your thirties is not the happy-go-lucky free-for-all it was when you were twenty-two and that the honest answer is more likely to be, 'Actually, last night my married lover appeared wearing suspenders and a darling little Angora crop-top, told me he was gay/a sex addict/a narcotic addict/a commitment phobic and beat me up with a dildo,' than, 'Super, thanks.'

Not being a natural liar, I ended up mumbling shamefacedly to Geoffrey, 'Fine,' at which point he boomed, 'So you *still* haven't got a feller!'

---

4. Write a short extract from your main character's diary.

Second person

Second person narratives are rare. Jamaica Kincaid uses the second person very effectively in a short story, 'Girl', in the form of giving advice/orders from mother to daughter. They have the unsettling effect of implicating the reader and are used in adventure game books whereby 'you' (the main character - hero) can choose what action you take. A very different usage can be found in parts of Iain Banks' novel, *Complicity* - not for the fainthearted - in which 'you' are doing the murdering. The second person often evokes a sense of trial as if we are hearing the closing statement of a prosecutor. It also has the effect of distancing the narrator from events - at least, from blame.

1. Read the following extract from *The Hazel Phase* by Ashley Stokes. What effect does the second person have here?

Extract from *The Hazel Phase* by Ashley Stokes

You've delivered the documents as The Don instructed. As she reads you keep fixed on the emerald glints of light in the gin bottle and the bubbles that jostle and gently rise in the tonic. You lose yourself in the wasps, their acute angle turns and zigzag circuits above the steel dish of lemon wedges that lies on the wicker garden table between the two of you. She's dressed for summertime and lounging, in shirt and bikini. Her glossy tanned legs are pressed together now. The tips of her white high-heeled shoes nudge each other. She caresses the edges of the papers fanned out on her knees. When she starts to cry, the skin at your cheekbones pinches. You light another B&H, take another sip of G&T to balk a smile. Can't stop thinking that a minute ago, before the legalese hit her, before she swished her legs shut, a fringe of hair peeped out from her magenta bikini bottoms. Even as she weeps, even as she's hurting, you can't snuff out the glow of privilege that you feel.

'Just do this for me,' The Don had said. 'I can't deal with her right now. She'll loop the loop. I won't get through to her. And you're great at buttering her up.'

You know why he wants this. You know the firm is up Shit Street. The housing slump. Negative equity. The pound is still shadowing the Deutschmark.

---

2. Write a paragraph in the second person from the point of view of a father accusing his son of committing a crime.

Third person

Out of all the viewpoints, this is the most complicated as there are many variations of the third person and, yet, the third person is the most common form of narration. We will try to keep the following explanations as simple as possible.

The first one to deal with is the omniscient narrative: the one we advise against. This is the author playing God, which means that he or she is able to dip into all the characters' minds, tell us what they are thinking and doing as well as reminding us what is going on in Iran, if necessary. This might sound like a good way forward, but an omniscient author can be a disaster. It was used a lot in the nineteenth century in the novels of George Elliot and Tolstoy, for example, but these days we are more questioning as readers: we want to know how the author knows that and we want the characters to solve their own problems. In the past, the authorial voice was an author's trademark. This is what writers often refer to as 'a voice' and this authorial voice was used to narrate story after story: Edgar Allen Poe, Mark Twain, William Faulkner and Graham Greene are good examples. Such a voice would be closer to the first person 'storyteller'. Nowadays though, writers tend to play more with ventriloquism and use different voices to narrate different stories depending on their characters. 'Voice' now is often used to refer to the character's voice.

Experienced writers can still create very effective omniscient narratives. They create a narrative voice which can mediate between characters and events but, unlike the narratives of George Elliot and Tolstoy, it is not didactic and does not pass judgement on the characters or events.

These days writers are more likely to opt for a third person restricted viewpoint. This means that the story is related from the point of view of one or more characters. It may be an intimate third person which would be closer to the first person and able to relate the character's thoughts. Or it may also be a detached third person which acts more as a camera and does not enter the character's thoughts. We see events, hear dialogue, observe the setting, and make guesses about what the characters are thinking. This point of view can work brilliantly in fairly short fiction. The intimate third person is more common though. Writers may choose to write only from one character's point of view or from multiple viewpoints. New chapters or asterisks are often used to denote a change in point of view. A story told from several points of view replaces the need for authorial comment.

> **Tip - In a short story it is recommended to keep to one character's point of view. What you should not do, is move from character to character whenever you feel fit – unless you are confident that you can do it well. One of the commonest signs of an inexperienced writer is inconsistency in handling point of view. To suddenly switch point of view to characters that do not play a large part in the narrative can propel the reader out of the story and can hurt a story badly.**

1. Read the following extracts from *Sense and Sensibility* and *Eclipse of the Sun*. Which one is omniscient and which one is third person restricted? What is the difference? See the **Appendix** for comment.

Extract from *Eclipse of the Sun* by Phil Whitaker, Phoenix House, 1997 (p. 33)

Rajesh put the journal down and got to his feet. He flicked the main light on, squinting momentarily in the glare. Squatting in front of his grandfather's trunk, he removed the framed photographs one by one, the silence fuelling his excitement. The last thing he placed on the stone floor was the brass vase with its jasmine stems; the fragrance grew strong as he moved the flowers. He pulled the cotton cloth off the trunk and sprung the catch. At some point in the future, strolling in the evening cool with his new wife, he would recount this for her. And they would laugh gently together, she perhaps touching his arm at the memory of the first words they exchanged; the moment they had both known.

Sumila was hungry. The ache in her stomach, the craving for food, compounded her misery. She gazed at the flickering screen in front of her, eyes following the little figures running this way and that. The television was often a source of wistful regret. Watching the singers, actresses, dancers, she would wonder how they had got to be where they were; whether she could have achieved something similar. Yet that night, she had no idea what she was watching, her thoughts elsewhere.

She was not used to the pace at which her day had passed. Usually her time was taken up with household tasks, either around the home or shopping in Nandrapur. Although there was always plenty to do, she was never aware of being hurried. Today had been different.

Extract from Jane Austen's *Sense and Sensibility*, Crown Publishers, Inc. 1981 (Chapter 11, p26)

Little had Mrs Dashwood or her daughters imagined, when they came first into Devonshire, that so many engagements would arise to occupy their time as shortly presented themselves, or that they should have such frequent invitations and such constant visitors as to leave them little leisure for serious employment. Yet such was the case. When Marianne was recovered, the schemes of amusements at home and abroad which Sir John had been previously forming were put in execution. The private balls at the Park then began; and parties on the water were made and accomplished as often as a showery October would allow. In every meeting of the kind, Willoughby was included; and the ease and familiarity which naturally attended these parties were exactly calculated to give increasing intimacy to his acquaintance with the Dashwoods, to afford him opportunity of witnessing the excellences of Marianne, of marking his animated admiration of her, and of receiving, in her behaviour to himself, the most pointed assurance of her affection.

Elinor could not be surprised at their attachment. She only wished that it were less openly shown, and once or twice did venture to suggest the propriety of some self-command to Marianne. But Marianne abhorred all concealment where no real disgrace could attend unreserved; and to aim at the restraint of sentiments which were not in themselves illaudable, appeared to her not merely an unnecessary effort, but a disgraceful subjection of reason to commonplace and mistaken notions. Willoughby thought the same; and their behaviour, at all times, was an illustration of their opinions.

2. Try this exercise in order to practise different 3rd person narratives. Write a similar paragraph but using each of the different forms of narrative. Imagine two people on their first date. (A **student example** is given in the **Appendix**.)

i) **Detached 3ʳᵈ person (objective – external POV)**
E.g. A man and a woman walked along the river.

ii) **Intimate 3ʳᵈ person (subjective – internal POV)**

iii) **Omniscient narrative**

Stream of consciousness

Stream of consciousness narratives can be first, second or third person narratives but will normally be in the present tense. It is a term coined by William James in *Principles of Psychology* (1890) to denote the flow of inner experiences and became popular with modernist writers, in particular James Joyce, Virginia Woolf and Marcel Proust. A classic example is Molly Bloom's reflections towards the end of *Ulysses* by James Joyce. It is also often described as 'interior monologue'.

1. Below is an example of 'stream of consciousness'. Who is the character? What do you think is going on?

Must get some bread while I'm out or else he'll be yelling that they're isn't any and I'm absolutely sick to death of his yelling the miserable bastard. And some milk while I'm there. Really I can't seem to do anything these days without him yelling and slamming the door and I must go to the chemist or maybe I should wait a few more days it's not going to make that much difference. But I would like to know because that would give him something else to yell about and I reckon that would be the final yell he would get the hell out then and good riddance. I'll be fine on my own. I have friends and people who care for me and I'd better get some paracetamol and some petrol - if I've got enough to get to the garage and I'd better go before it gets dark I hate the winter and now look at the rain. And who knows maybe he will come and stay with me so I wouldn't be on my own. Where's my keys? I'd like that. But he's hardly likely to leave her is he and mustn't forget to post this letter. And buy some bread.

2. Write an interior monologue from the point of view of your main character.

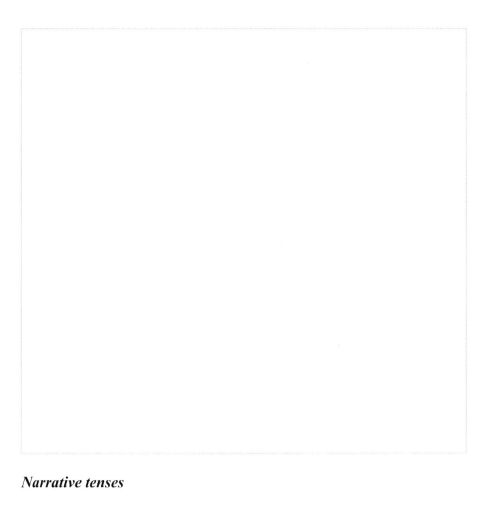

Narrative tenses

Which tense you choose to use will depend on from where you're telling the story. The choice is really only between past and present as the future tense is rarely used except in short passages. The majority of stories are narrated in the past tense but many contemporary writers choose to use the present tense (particularly with the first person) as it produces an illusion of events related as they happen and gives the narrative a sense of urgency and immediacy (i.e. Helen Fielding's *Bridget Jones' diary* - although note now the narrator smoothly moves into the recent past).

> **Tip - If you are using the past tense and narrating another time in the past which would normally necessitate the use of the past perfect (i.e. 'She had gone to see him'), try not to use too many 'hads' as it has the effect of distancing the reader.**

1. Read through the above extracts again. Make a note of which extract uses which tense.

Lolita

Bridget Jones' Diary

The Hazel Phase

Sense and Sensibility

Eclipse of the Sun

2. Write a section of your own work in the present tense.

Assignment: Changing point of view

For this assignment, either rewrite a section of your story from another character's viewpoint or change the form of narrative at sentence level. For example, if you are writing in the third person, try writing in the first person. If you choose this option, try not to simply change the pronouns but the entire narrative approach - hopefully, you will find you need to anyway.

> **Tip - It is useful to experiment with different points of view, explore tenses and ways of telling a story. Remember though, that these are experiments, ways of practising your craft, and may not be the best option.**

PART 3 – ENDS

The Rewrite

This is the final step (at least, staircase) of writing - and the steepest. Here we consider what is good and bad writing, discuss the importance of redrafting, editing, and of giving and receiving feedback.

1. Murdering your darlings

Before murdering your dearest sentences sharpen your pencil and practise the following:

Word warm up

1. Write a half page of prose, allowing yourself no more than 1 adjective and 1 adverb (an adjective is a word that describes a noun i.e. 'beautiful' while an adverb modifies a verb i.e. 'beautifully'). Take a broad topic such as 'The Sea' and describe it. The main practical outcome of this exercise is the development (possibly unconscious) of the use of metaphor, as well as to find new ways of describing using verbs and nouns.

So, what is good writing?

A tricky one. Or is it? There are always critics who complain that a particular writer is too obtuse and difficult, or too facile, or too descriptive, or too economical, and so on. We only have to compare the brief passages from **Angela Carter and Raymond Carver** (see **Appendix**) to see how different writing styles can be. But the key here is *style*. You may not like a writer's particular style, but that does not necessarily make it bad writing. Similarly, you may not like the story, but neither does that necessarily mean it is badly written. Bad writing is vague, generalised, over written in parts, employs bad grammar, only *tells* us what is happening, and is often clichéd: bad writing either over-simplifies or fails to present us with a clear picture of the story.

George Orwell writes that, 'One can write nothing readable unless one constantly struggles to efface one's own personality. Good prose is like a windowpane.' *Why I Write*, 1947

We have already discussed the role of the author in Part 2, but the idea that good prose should be as clear and as vivid as if we were watching through a window is a helpful analogy.

Modes of writing

In order to ensure that we write well, we need to think about how writing works. Generally, we use three modes of writing to tell our stories:

Narration (outlining what is happening)
Description (colouring in setting/characters)
Dialogue (breathing life into the characters)

All these modes work together to create a story. It is important to vary the modes of writing in order to keep the writing interesting. Miles of description can be boring while clear cut lines of pure narration will not provide the depth which we need to engage with the characters. Dialogue alone can not tell the complete story.

Another way to think of writing is in terms of *Scene* and *Summary*. A scene places the reader in the action while summary can bypass several years/events.

1. Select any piece of fiction and think carefully about narration, description and dialogue. Which parts are scenes? Which are summary?

Pacing

Pacing is also enormously important. Different readers prefer different paces and, again, different genres reflect this. However, a well written story will use both telescopic and microscopic scenes, include fast paced action and dialogue combined with slower more reflective moments. The language, the length of the sentences, the detail (or lack of it) should mirror the scene you are describing. To vary the pace of the writing is a difficult thing to do and one which takes a lot of practice.

Show, don't tell

This has become a mantra in creative writing, and one which is worth chanting every morning. Generally, it means that you must show us how a character feels, rather than tell us. If a character is angry, how can you show that? Rather than say 'Josh was angry', you could try: 'Josh clenched his fist/slammed the door/threw his coat down/stomped out of the room' and so on. If a character is cold she could rub her feet, breathe on her hands, shiver… If a character is a manic depressive, he could stuff himself with chocolate. And so on. The key is to think laterally, and not literally. Showing is about the action and reaction of characters to specific events and emotions.

Usually it helps to set as many scenes as you can. Do not summarise or narrate at great length. But there is a danger here of being simplistic because, even when narrating, it is possible to use language which shows and not tells. For example, adjectives and adverbs often tell rather than show (see below) while the past perfect tense and passive forms can kill a reader's interest in what happened. Compare the following sentences:

i) She was hit by the laundry van.

ii) The laundry van hit her.

iii) 'Shit!' she cried as the laundry van came straight towards her.

The first sentence is passive. It is slow and long winded. Despite the unfortunate accident, the sentence itself carries little impact. The second sentence is active, therefore we know immediately what hit her. The result is more hard-hitting and should be used if summarising events. The third sentence is part of a scene and therefore more immediate: we see the character's reaction to an event. This is a very simple example of showing.

---

1. The following passage is a basic example of telling and not showing. Have a go at rewriting it in order to show more. (There are a couple of *student examples* in the **Appendix**.)

Fiona left the restaurant angry and resentful. She walked down the street passing her old school on the left. It was cold so she wrapped her scarf around her neck. She reached the bus stop and halted suddenly. She imagined all the nasty things she would say to him.

Someone beeped insistently at her from across the road. She looked across and saw a friend who worked at the restaurant. The friend wound down the window and asked her where she was going and if she wanted a lift. Fiona smiled falsely, shook her head and made an excuse. Her friend asked if she was all right before driving off.

It began raining. Before long, water streamed along the pavement, forming fast little rivulets along the road. Torrents of water headed for the drains, gushing and gurgling as it cascaded down. In the skies steel and grey storm clouds gathered overhead. It looked like it was never going to stop raining.

Beware of 'telling' in dialogue

We have already covered how to write dialogue in Part 2, but it is worth saying that while dialogue is generally considered to be the purest form of 'showing' in fiction, this is not always the case. One thing you do not want to do is to tell all in dialogue. This is what is known as being overly expositional (i.e. giving too much away).

1. Consider this scene. Roger is on a train going to Birmingham where he was born.

'Is this yours?' a middle aged woman asked Roger, picking up a copy of The Daily Mail that had been left on the seat next to him.

'No,' Roger replied. 'It must have been the previous passenger's.'

'How far you going then?' The woman sat down, resting a red leather bag on her lap.

'Birmingham.'

'Oh what's there then? Not many tourist attractions, wouldn't have thought?'

'I was born there, apparently. My parents left when I was two

years old and we went to live in Nottingham and then Doncaster where I went to school. After that we moved to London – Shepherd's Bush and then I got a job in banking in the city, working for Barclays. I used to have grandparents in Birmingham and I've always wanted to revisit so I decided when I had a spare weekend I would go.'

'Well, I hope you aren't disappointed.'

We are almost immediately given a synopsis of the character's past and present. There is no element of surprise or tension. How would you improve it?

Metaphors and Similes

We use metaphors and similes everyday and they should be an integral part of your writing.

A metaphor is something that describes something laterally, not literally. For example, 'She is a tower of strength.' She is not literally a tower of strength. Metaphors may appear as verbs (a talent may *blossom)* or as adjectives (a novice may be *green)*

A well-known metaphor can also become an idiomatic phrase (for example, 'not see the wood for the trees' or 'going against the grain').

Such idioms can be a useful shortcut to saying what we want to say but when we no longer think about the meaning, it is no longer an effective metaphor. A metaphor which is overused becomes a dead metaphor or a cliché (for example, 'the end of the day'). Our job as writers is to think of fresh and imaginative metaphors - but always keeping within the limitations of the narrative voice (if you are telling the story through the eyes of a ninety year old man you need to use the kind of metaphors and similes he would use).

Tip - A metaphor can be used symbolically to illustrate the theme of a story. For example, reference to a lost toy could allude to the theme of growing up. But careful not to make your metaphors too contrived or clichéd - e.g. a red rose symbolising love.

Similes are similar to metaphors except they use 'as' or 'like' and are not always as strong.

Compare 'He is a rat' (metaphor) to 'He is like a rat' (simile).

Where possible, use a metaphor and cut straight to the image.

1. Have a look at some original similes by **Raymond Chandler** and metaphors by **Helen Cross** in the **Appendix**. Write a couple of your own similes and metaphors.

2. Listen to the radio or the TV for an hour. How many clichés/dead metaphors can you count? Write them down. Any original ones?

> **Tip** - Too many metaphors and similes can have a negative effect. Your writing may come across as overwritten and 'purple'. Make sure your metaphors are well chosen, sparingly placed, and appropriate to the voice of the character.

Rewrite, rewrite, rewrite

There are very few writers who claim not to rework and edit their writing. Most rewrite many times. Extensive planning can cut down on the amount of revision we have to do, but stories rarely go perfectly to plan (and it is also important not to be too controlling) so always be prepared to rewrite. It can be difficult to delete dazzling sentences, or even an entire first page, but sometimes it is necessary in order to make your story more fluent and wordtight. As Sir Arthur Quiller-Couch said, 'Whenever you feel an impulse to perpetrate a piece of exceptionally fine writing, obey it - whole-heartedly - and delete it before sending your manuscripts to press. *Murder your darlings.*' (*The Art of Writing,* 1916)

Before we begin, it is important to note that there are two main parts to revision:

1. **THE BIG PICTURE (story composition). This focuses on the visible anatomy of the work - the structure, the characters, the conflict, the pacing, the setting, the dialogue and the overall plausibility. You need to make sure every scene is necessary. Chekhov writes that, 'If you say in the first chapter that there is a rifle hanging on the wall, in the second or third chapter it absolutely must go off. If it's not going to be fired, it shouldn't be hanging there.' This is known as Chekhov's gun and serves to illuminate the importance of every detail. If something is not serving a purpose then it shouldn't be there. If a character is not playing a role, get rid of him or her. If a scene is not moving the story forward, get rid of it. If the dialogue is telling us nothing about either character or plot, delete it. The chances are these unnecessary scenes will be boring. As Elmore Leonard said, 'leave out the bits reader tend to skip' (see below). If nothing is happening in your story, think of Raymond Chandler's advice, 'When in doubt, have a man come through the door with a gun in his hand.' He was**

referring to detective fiction but the point remains the same – you need to engage the reader at all times. The effect of a man or woman with a gun is that it immediately creates tension.

2. **THE DETAIL (the writing). This is a microscopic examination of the language used. When revising the writing beware of the following:**

♦ **Adjectival and adverbial pileups.** Too many adjectives (e.g. soft) and adverbs (e.g. softly) can make writing seem overwritten. It also has the effect of 'telling' us how a character feels/acts rather than showing us. Try to use more verbs that replace the need for adjectives and adverbs.

♦ **Passive sentences.** Compare 'The axe was sharpened by Arthur' and 'Arthur sharpened the axe'. As with the van incident, the first sentence is passive - the subject of the sentence is having something done to it which makes it more wordy and potentially more abstract. The second sentence is active - the subject of the sentence is doing the action and therefore more immediate and engaging. Always try to use active verbs - make the verb muscle the sentence. How else can you say 'is' and 'was'?

♦ **Abstractions/vagueness**. Although an image may be perfectly clear to you, to the reader, it may be abstract. 'She washed the shrunken wrinkled green sheets, layered them into the oval terracotta dish and decorated them with slices of iced cool eyes and pebble sized blood red tomatoes.' (cf. 'She made a salad.') Tell it as it is - unless it is a stylistic device.

♦ **Clichés.** Your writing should stand out, be original, not 'old hat'.

♦ **Generalisations.** Where possible, be specific - opt for precise detail rather than general description.

♦ **Bad grammar.** When you are writing, you can turn off all the automatic features and write whatever - and however - you want. But when you are editing you must check your work for grammatical and spelling errors. ***Be careful of writing 'its' for it's (it is), 'there' for they're (they are)*** and so on. Also try to avoid too many exclamation marks - your writing should exclaim for you. If you are unsure about some aspects of English grammar invest in a grammar book (Michael Swan's *Practical English Usage,* OUP) is aimed at EFL students but nevertheless provides a good all round overview).

- **One paced.** Try to make sure there is variation in the pacing of the writing. Zoom in on some parts and zoom back in others. Balance dialogue with description.

- **Telling too much.** Wave that axe about: show the reader you're angry, don't tell us.

> **Tip - For some excellent advice on writing, have a look at Elmore Leonard's Ten Rules of writing published in 'Easy on the Adverbs, Exclamation points & Especially Hooptedoodle'** *Writers on Writing, Volume 11,* **(Times Books, 2003)**
> **See www.nytimes.com/books/special/writers.htm**

1. Try to read as much as you can. Practise reading as a writer. Select a passage of fiction and look for any of the above 'mistakes'. How do authors avoid them?

2. Select a page of your own writing and take out all the adjectives and adverbs. Find other ways of description.

3. Choose a published piece of work that you know is not to your taste, and find ten things to praise in the writing. Be specific: give examples.

4. Look at the criteria in *Revise your own work* in the **Appendix.** Apply the criteria to your own work.

Punctuation

Punctuation is used to help clarify the meaning of your writing, particularly comma usage. Comma usage can be complex and, indeed, personal. Many editors argue about its 'correct' usage but there are some basic rules you can follow. Commas are used either to separate a part of the sentence about the subject that could otherwise be deleted, or to add extra information about the subject. For example:

Zora stood in the queue for hours, arms folded, waiting for someone to serve her.

Zora stood in the queue for hours, arms folded.

Now compare the following sentences:

The man who sells me lottery tickets says that I am unlucky.
Dan, the man who sells lottery tickets, says that I am unlucky.

In the first example, the sentence would be incomplete without the identifying clause (i.e. 'The man says that I am unlucky - what man?) The second sentence is adding extra information about the subject and could easily exist without it.

Commas are used to separate adjectives when qualifying a noun (e.g. 'the large, middle-aged woman') unless an adjective is qualifying another adjective ('a bright green shirt').

They are also used to differentiate between different subjects. Compare the following two sentences:

'What do you know about Luis?'
'What do you think about, Luis?'

The subject of each sentence is different, therefore the meaning is different. In the first sentence 'Luis' is the subject, in the second 'you' is the subject.

There is a tendency for beginning writers to use run-on sentences. For example:

As she walks down the road, I feel small and insignificant, just another tick on her call out sheet, I should have offered her coffee.

The first comma is not necessary as 'I' is the subject of the sentence. 'Just another tick' is adding extra information and therefore separated by a comma, and the last part of the sentence should be separated by a full-stop.

As she walks down the road I feel small and insignificant, just another tick on her call out sheet. I should have offered her coffee.

Question tags such as 'isn't it?' and 'aren't there?' should be preceded by a comma.

'This is the right way to use a comma, isn't it?'

On a line from A to D, A represents a comma, B a semi-colon, C a colon and D a full-stop. A dash is an informal colon (and becoming more common) while semi-colons and colons seem to be used less - particularly by American writers.

Tip - Experienced writers play with commas and punctuation (for example, Gabriel Garcia Marquez in *Autumn of the Patriarch* uses run-on sentences throughout, employing only one full stop in the first chapter, two in the second etc.) But, for beginning writers it is advisable to keep sentences simple. Always think about the subject, verb and object.

Layout of text and dialogue

The presentation of your writing is very important: an experienced reader can often spot a beginning writer by the layout of the text and dialogue. Therefore, it is worthwhile spending time formatting your text. The most important thing is to be consistent. It is usual though to left align the first paragraph of a short story or new chapter and, subsequently, indent all following paragraphs. Some publishers indent by a tab-key, others by four spaces. **Dialogue should be indented in the same way as a new paragraph.** Single speech marks are generally favoured by British publishers (speech within speech would then be double). Double speech marks are used for US publications (single for speech within speech). All punctuation marks (usually) go inside speech. Each new speaker should start on a new line and so should the character reacting to the speech (even if he doesn't say anything). Speech marks are not necessary for thoughts. You can use them but if you are telling the story through the character, you don't really need them. Spacing should be 1.5 in manuscripts. For example:

Chapter 1

'I probably shouldn't be telling you this, but I overheard something very odd last night at Ricky's,' Sheena said, handing him a cup of coffee. Strong. Sweet. Just how he liked it.

'Yeah?' He took the coffee and balanced it on the arm of the chair and unfolded the paper. He slipped his glasses up his nose.

84

She crossed her arms and looked down at his balding head. The temples were beginning to look like the patchwork on a football. He really should want to know.

'Yeah,' she said, walking back towards the kitchen.

'What was that then?' he said, and yawned loudly.

She knew he was faking. She looked back at him. He was still pretending to read the paper.

'There was a woman there who said that she had seen you climb out of a window in Samson's Alley,' she said.

The paper tore slightly as he turned a page.

'Rubbish. How did this woman know it was me?'

'She said, "I swear it was that man who works in the pharmacy. A dark man, wears glasses round his neck, always very helpful." That's you, isn't it?'

An exception would be texts online (because of HTML) which left align all text and leave a line between paragraphs/speech.

Sharing practice

However good we get at editing our own work, there comes a point when it can be extremely useful to have some external feedback. Professional writers have agents and editors to give them feedback and to edit their work (although this is not something to depend on and it is increasingly difficult to find more hands-on editors). For beginning writers, it is harder. Whatever you do, don't be tempted to ask your mother, partner or best friend - unless they happen to be writers themselves. An ideal critic is someone who is studying, or has studied, writing fiction/literature.

Giving feedback - It is important when giving feedback to be positive and constructive. Try to focus on two things that you like/think work well and one thing which you think could be improved. Use the *Revise your own work* criteria to help you.

Receiving feedback - Sometimes it can be hard to hear someone say that anything in your work could be improved. However, you must listen and make notes. Let a person have their say. If you find yourself trying to justify your work, or having to explain it, then maybe it isn't working as well as you thought. There will be times when you will not agree with a person's comments. You may be right. If possible, ask someone else. If more than one person says the same thing, then you need to do something about it. However, if the advice is conflicting, then this is where your judgement needs to step in. Ultimately, it is your work and it may well be that the reader does simply not like your approach or style.

'The extent to which we agree with a writer about life in general is the unacknowledged X-factor in our critical response. People who declare that an author has failed to achieve excellence may, in truth, be put off by the author's sunny optimism, chronic gloom, deeply held beliefs, nihilism, whatever.' Michael Faber in a review of *Notes from a Turkish Whorehouse*, Guardian Review, 04.03.06

> **Tip - When giving or receiving feedback it is important to establish whether this is an early draft or a more final draft. If it is an early draft it is more helpful to focus on the story composition rather than on the detail such as grammar.**

Writers' swap shop

If possible, find someone you can swap your work with. Make sure you agree on a word limit. To begin with, 1000 words would be reasonable. Arrange a day and a time to discuss your work. This could either be face-to-face or electronically. Try to get into the habit of doing this on a monthly basis.

Assignment: writing critiques

For this assignment, if you don't have a writing partner or belong to a writers' group, choose a story (online or printed) and write approximately half a page of comments, focusing on the story composition and the detail. Or perhaps you can join in an online forum and post your own story as well as offer your comments on someone else's work. If you do have a writing partner then exchange your work. Make sure you start off on a positive note and end on a positive note. Use the *Revise your own work* criteria as a guide.

2. Beginnings and Endings

'What we call the beginning is often the end
And to make an end is to make a beginning.
The end is where we start from.'
TS Eliot, 1942, *Four Quartets*, 'Little Gidding', pt. 5

Finally, this last section will look at various ways of beginning and ending, casting hooks and twisting tales.

Word warm up

> 1. Write several opening sentences. They can be about anything at all. Which ones have the most potential? Why?

1. Beginnings

You may be wondering why we haven't looked at beginnings in the beginning. There are a couple of reasons. Firstly because beginnings are one of the hardest things to write so it would be unfair to ask you to write a brilliant opening as an initial exercise. Most people before reading an entire story will read at least the first paragraph, at most the first page, before they decide whether or not they will continue. Therefore, the first paragraph must capture the reader and make sure he or she stays put. The other reason is that beginnings are often something we write, or rewrite, at the end when we are absolutely sure of the ending.

What should a beginning do?

1. Read the following openings from the novels: *1984, Girl with a Pearl Earring and Life of Pi*. Study them carefully. How effective are the openings? Do you want to read on? Why? Make notes on what each of them does. For brief commentaries on the openings and titles see the **Appendix**.

Opening of *1984* by George Orwell, Penguin, 1983 (1st published in 1949)

1

It was a bright cold day in April, and the clocks were striking thirteen. Winston Smith, his chin nuzzled into his breast in an effort to escape the vile wind, slipped quickly through the glass doors of Victory Mansions, though not quickly enough to prevent a swirl of gritty dust from entering along with him.

The hallway smelt of boiled cabbage and old rag mats. At one end of it a coloured poster, too large for indoor display, had been tacked to the wall. It depicted simply an enormous face, more than a metre wide: the face of a man of about forty-five, with a heavy black moustache and ruggedly handsome features. Winston made for the stairs. It was no use trying the lift. Even at the best of times it was seldom working, and at present the electric current was cut off during daylight hours. It was part of the economy drive in preparation for Hate Week. The flat was seven flights up, and Winston, who was thirty-nine and had a varicose ulcer above his right ankle, went slowly, resting several times on the way. On each landing, opposite the lift-shaft, the poster with the enormous face gazed from the wall. It was one of those pictures which are so contrived that the eyes follow you about when you move. BIG BROTHER IS WATCHING YOU, the caption beneath it ran.

Opening of *Girl with a Pearl Earring* by Tracy Chevalier, HarperCollins Publishers, 1999

1664

My mother did not tell me they were coming. Afterwards she said she did not want me to appear nervous. I was surprised, for I thought she knew me well. Strangers would think I was calm. I did not cry as a baby. Only my mother would note the tightness along my jaw, the widening of my already wide eyes.

I was chopping vegetables in the kitchen when I heard voices outside our front door - a woman's, bright as polished brass, and a man's, low and dark like the wood of the table I was working on. They were the kind of voices we heard rarely in our house. I could hear rich carpets in their voices, books and pearls and fur.

Opening from *Life of Pi* by Yann Martel, Canongate, 2002

CHAPTER 1

My suffering left me sad and gloomy.

Academic study and the steady, mindful practice of religion slowly brought me back to life. I have kept up what some people would consider my strange religious practices. After one year of high school, I attended the University of Toronto and took a double-major Bachelor's degree. My majors were religious studies and zoology. My fourth-year thesis for religious studies concerned aspects of the cosmogony theory of Isaac Lucia, the great sixteenth-century Kabbalist from Safed. My zoology thesis was a functional analysis of the thyroid gland of the three-toed sloth. I chose the sloth because its demeanour - calm, quiet and introspective - did something to soothe my shattered self.

2. When you have finished, compare your notes to *Hooking the reader* in the **Appendix.** These extracts are from longer fiction. Are short story openings any different?

3. Read again the openings of the two short stories you have looked at on this course and also several other openings of short stories. Do they meet the criteria outlined in *Hooking the reader*?

4. Read through the following opening lines from novels. Do you know where they are from? It doesn't matter if you don't - in fact, it may be more fun. Continue writing one of them - at least, the first paragraph.

i)   Mr and Mrs Dursley, of number four, Privet Drive, were proud to say that they were perfectly normal, thank you very much.

ii)   It was love at first sight.

iii)   'Now, what I want is, Facts.'

iv)   She only stopped screaming when she died.

v)   There was no possibility of taking a walk that day.

vi)   It is cold at six-forty in the morning of a March day in Paris, and seems even colder when a man is about to be executed by firing squad.

vii)   The corpse without hands lay in the bottom of a small sailing dinghy drifting just within sight of the Suffolk coast.

viii)   They departed, the gods, on the day of the strange tide.

To find out the authors of these opening lines and the titles of the
books go to the **Appendix**.

> **Tip - Do you really really need those first couple of paragraphs? Wouldn't you be better off opening your story further on in the story? Any crucial information can be threaded in later. Helen Simpson in an article on Virginia Woolf and Katherine Mansfield in the Guardian writes that 'Chekhov himself claimed that whenever he finished a story, he cut the first and last paragraphs' – hence the tortoise effect. 'Little Writ Large', Guardian, February 15, 2003**

Titles

The title of your story is also paramount. The best titles are catchy, sometimes unusual, and reflect either the theme, the character and/or the story itself. *1984* implies (or, at least, implied) a futuristic novel. *A Girl With a Pearl Earring* is the title of the painting by Vermeer that inspired Tracy Chevalier and *Life of Pi* suggests a fantastic life and journey. Many writers struggle to find the right title. Famously, F. Scott Fitzgerald was going to call *The Great Gatsby* 'Trimalchio in West Egg' which doesn't quite have the same ring.

1. Take an earlier plot or story outline and give it a title.

2. Write down a couple of potential titles and make some notes as to what they might be about.

3. What is the title of your story? How does it reflect the story?

2. Endings

'I always write my last lines, my last paragraph, my last page first, and then I go back and work towards it.' Katherine Anne Porter, 'Katherine Anne Porter: An Interview', *Paris Review*, XXIX (1963)

Not everyone works like this, but the quote illustrates the importance of the end of the story. This is payoff time and your reader wants to feel satisfied. In today's fiction, endings need not be conclusive, they need not be happy, they should not be moralistic (the thief getting his hand accidentally-or-on-purpose severed) and they need not be an end at all: you may choose to end on an image, or a mood: something which reflects the *theme* of the story. The important thing is that there is a change in the story, usually in the character. The best endings are surprising but, on reflection, inevitable. A twist in the tale can be very effective if it genuinely surprises the reader. As a general note of precaution, be careful of killing off your main character (an exception to this is Tobias Wolff's 'Bullet in the Brain'). Unless you have framed the story in such a way as to set up a narrator, the death of the main character is less effective: who then would be telling the story?

'One might say that the short story is essentially "end-oriented", inasmuch as one begins a short story in the expectation of soon reaching its conclusion, whereas one embarks upon a novel with no very precise idea of when one will finish it.' *The Art of Fiction*, David Lodge (Penguin, 1992)

> **Tip - Whatever you do, do not have the main character wake up to discover it was all a dream/nightmare. This is what is known as a 'flat' or cheat ending.**

Twisting the tale

Twists in tales are always popular although, due to reader expectations, they can be hard to do well as twisting devices are limited. You may choose to have a hero who is really a villain, or vice versa, or use the device of misunderstanding: a character goes through the whole story believing one thing when she/he has misheard. A character could strive towards a particular goal, only to be revealed that it is a false goal and the true objective is something else.

Whichever you choose, it is important to be absolutely convincing in your deception: the more convincing you are, the more surprising the ending will be.

1. To create a twist you really do have to know the end. Your aim is to deceive the reader all the way through until the end. Events and characters have to be not what they seem. Have a read through Roald Dahl's 'Lamb to the Slaughter' online or any of his Tales of the Unexpected. In 'Lamb to the Slaughter', Mary, at first, is established as a loving wife but ends up giggling over the fact that the officers have eaten the weapon which she used to kill her husband.

2. Have a go at mapping out a story with a twist in the tale. You may even want to write it up at some point. There is a fairly big market for twist in the tale stories. Many women's magazines such as Bella, Best, Reader's Digest and Woman's Weekly publish short stories with surprise endings (1000 – 2000 words). My Weekly, MsLexia, The London Magazine accept stories. Try the website twistinthetale.com

The End and Final Assignment: The Completed Story

This is almost the end of the workbook and you should, hopefully, have completed a 2,000 word story - and much more. We hope you have enjoyed working through this *Writing Fiction Workbook*.

For information on publishing the writers' bible is *The Writers' & Artists' Yearbook* (published annually by A & C Black publishers). There are also many hundreds of e-publishers and now that print on demand technology has advanced it is finally possible to self publish work without incurring enormous costs. You need to feel comfortable about publishing your work and it is not recommended for beginning writers but, for those who have more experience and fall outside the mainstream for whatever reason, or for those who like to have more control over their work, it is now an attractive option.

We recommend Lulu (www.lulu.com) which also gives you the opportunity of publishing just for yourself, as well as to sell to the public, and you only pay for the cost of each book - typically between $14 - $19 (£8 - £12) depending on length and profit margin. (Hence it is now possible to publish novellas - something publishers would refuse because they weren't financially viable.) Beware though: in order to sell your book you need to think about marketing and on your own you have very limited resources.

Below are other useful websites for reading, writing, ideas, research and publishing:

Reading links

For short stories online. Some websites allow you to post your own.

Short Stories	**www.short-stories.co.uk**
Classic Reader	**www.classicreader.com**
Richmond Review	**www.richmondreview.co.uk/library**
Project Gutenberg	**www.gutenberg.net**

Writing links

For agents, publishers, writing tips, competitions, awards etc.

Author Network	**www.author-network.com**
BBC Get Writing	**http://bbc.co.uk/dna/getwriting/**
Writing Corner	**www.writingcorner.com**
Bloomsbury	**www.bloomsbury.com**
Short Story	**www.shortstory.com**
Flash Fiction	**www.shortshortshort.com**
Booktrust	**www.booktrust.org.uk**

There are several magazines about writing, some of which accept stories for publication and/or hold competitions: Writing Magazine, Writers' News (**www.writersnews.co.uk**), Writers' Forum, Stand Magazine, MsLexia, Springboard, Poets & Writers (**www.pw.org**), The Fix and Critical Quarterly.

Starting points

Real life stories, images and characters all make good starting points.

Home Truths	**www.bbc.co.uk/radio4/hometruths/**
Images	**www.cheap-poster.com**
Characters	**www.npg.org.uk**

Help with research

Help with news, words, dates, geography, science and people.

Personality Types	**www.personalitypage.com/home.htm**
Dying words	**www.corsinet.com/braincandy/dying.htm**
World wide words	**www.quinion.com/words**
Virtual Calendar	**www.vpcalendar.net**
British Council	**www.britishcouncil.org/home**
National Geographic	**www.nationalgeographic.com**
History	**www.historychannel.com**
Nature (Science)	**www.nature.com**
Encyclopaedia	**http://enwikipedia.org/wiki**

A short short story reading list

Byatt, AS, *The Matisse Stories*, (Vintage, 1994)
Carter, Angela, *The Bloody Chamber*, (Penguin, 1987)
Carver, Raymond, *Where I'm Calling From* (Harvill, 1993)
Chekhov, AP, *Lady With Lapdog & Other Stories* (Penguin, 1964)
Gogol, Nikolai, *The Complete Tales of Gogol* (Chatto, 1985)
Hammick, Georgina, *People for Lunch and Spoilt*, (Vintage, London, 1996)
Maitland, Sara, *Women Fly When Men Aren't Watching* (Virago, 1992)
McEwan, Ian, *First Love, Last Rites* (Picador, 1976)
Munro, Alice, *Selected Stories*, (Vintage, 1997)
Oates, Joyce Carol, *Them, Black Water and Stories*
Wilson, Angus, *Collected Short Stories,* (Penguin, 1994)

Other recommended short story writers: Katherine Mansfield, Flannery O'Connor, Guy de Maupassant, William Faulkner, Sean O'Faolain, Gabriel Garcia Marquez, Grace Paley, Lorrie Moore, Joyce Carol Oates, E.Annie Proulx, Martin Amis, Irvine Welsh, Tobias Wolff, William Trevor, Toby Litt and Helen Simpson.

Critical Works on Writing Fiction

Aristotle, *Poetics*, (Penguin, 1996)
Bell, J & Magrs, P (eds) *The Creative Writing Coursebook*, (Macmillan, 2001)
Booth, Wayne, *The Rhetoric of Fiction*, (University of Chicago Press, 1961)
Chatman, S, *Story and Discourse: Narrative Structure in Fiction and Film*, (Cornell University Press, 1978)
Goldberg, N, *Writing Down the Bones*, (Shambhala, 1986)
King, Stephen, *On Writing*, (Hodder & Stoughton, 2000)
Lerner, B, *The Forest for the Trees*, (Macmillan, 2002)
Lodge, David, *The Art of Fiction*, (Penguin, 1992)
McKee, Robert, *Story*, (Methuen, 1998)
Singleton, J, Luckhurst, M (eds.) *The Creative Writing Handbook*, (Macmillan Press Ltd. 1996)
Sheriff, John Paxton, *Practical Short Story Writing*, (Hale, 1995)
Stein, Sol, *Stein on Writing* (St. Martin's Press, 1995)

Appendix

Part 1

Sources for stories

Any of the following can be used to collect stories. When something interesting catches your eye, try to get into the habit of jotting it down in your notebook.

- Newspapers and magazines (particularly tabloids and local newspapers) General news, human interest, gossip, obituaries, exclusives, news in brief, lonely hearts...
- Radio programmes (e.g. 'Home Truths')
- Television documentaries
- Myths, legends and folk tales
- History
- Literature/film
- Theatre/dance
- Family stories
- Local gossip
- Memory/Experience
- Dreams
- Photographs
- Music
- Observations of people and events
- Imagination

To write what you know?

Maeve Binchy: I would advise anyone to write as they speak, and on the subjects that they know about. (quoted from www.authorsontheweb.com)

This is something that writers have debated over and over. Some schools of thought insist that you should only write what you know. Graham Swift says, 'I could not agree with anything less. My maxim would be for God's sake write about what you don't know! For how else will you bring your imagination into play? How else will you discover or explore anything.' (quoted from *The Creative Writing Handbook*, Macmillan Press, 1996, p101) He has a point. A writer who only writes what he or she knows will be very limited. But it does depend on what you are writing. If you are writing fantasy, then almost anything goes as long as it works within its own laws of reality and here the imagination has few limitations. On the other hand, if you are writing realistic fiction and you happen to be a rich, white public schoolboy from London, you are less likely to write convincingly from the point of view of an uneducated Hispanic kid from the Bronx. Less likely, but not impossible. This is where research and, indeed, observation come in. However, if you don't have time to spend living in the Bronx, you may choose to write something which is closer to your field of experience.

As we have said a writer needs experience, observation, imagination and research. Writing is a blending of these strands. You will probably find it easier to lean more heavily on your own experiences to begin with but, as you gain in confidence and ability, you will be able to move beyond the arena of your own experience. Just remember that, whether it is 'true' or not, it must be believable.

Graham Swift writes that: 'One of the fundamental aims of fiction is to enable us to enter, imaginatively, experiences other than our own.' (*ibid*)

And remember that we experience the same emotions - albeit, perhaps, to different events. Chekhov wrote that, 'Everything I learned about human nature I learned from me.' (quoted from *Story* by Robert McKee (Methuen, 1999, p386)

Some definitions of a short story

Edgar Allan Poe (1809-49)
Guy de Maupassant (1850-93)
Anton Chekhov (1860-1904)
'These writers evolved the qualities especially associated with the short story: close texture, unity of mood, suggestive idiom, economy of means.'
(Ed. Linda Williams, *Bloomsbury Guides to English Literature,* Bloomsbury, 1992)

'A short story will normally concentrate on a single event with only one or two characters, more economically than a novel's sustained exploration of social background.'
(Chris Baldick, *Concise Dictionary of Literary Terms,* OUP, 1991)

'At once a parable and a slice of life, at once symbolic and real, both a valid picture of some phase of experience, and a sudden illumination of one of the perennial, moral and psychological paradoxes which lie at the heart of *la condition humaine.*'
(John Bayley, *The Short Story: Henry James to Elizabeth Bowen*, Palgrave Macmillan, 1988)

'Many contemporary stories can also seem cruel by nature, like fairy stories, yet far from naïve: based instead on a formula which combines sophistication with sensationalism. Whatever their length they also seem to advertise their brevity, as much as their 'purity'. By contrast, the great masters of the form - Chekhov or Joyce or Henry James; Kafka or Kipling or Lawrence - seem to have all the time in the world for their stories, a leisureliness in which the reader can relax and look around.'
(John Bayley *ibid*)

Nadine Gordimer writes that, '[The short story is] a highly specialised and skilful form, closer to poetry.'
(Quoted from Susan Lohafer, *Coming to Terms with the Short Story,* Louisiana State University Press, 1983)

'I do not feel that the short story can be, or should be, used for the analysis or development of character... The short story, as I see it to be, allows for what is crazy about humanity; obstinacies, inordinate heroisms, "immortal longings."'
Elizabeth Bowen, *Afterthought: Pieces about Writing*, Hardback Longmans, 1962)

'... the short story can be anything the author decides it to be; it can be anything from the death of the horse to a young girl's first love affair, from the static sketch without plot to the swiftly moving machine of bold action and climax, from the prose poem, painted rather than written, to the piece of straight reportage in which style, colour, and elaboration have no place, from the piece which catches like a cobweb the light, subtle iridescence of emotions that can never really be captured to the solid tale in which all emotion, all action, all reaction is measured, fixed, puttied, glazed, and finished, like a well-built house, with three coats of shining and enduring paint. In the infinite flexibility, indeed, lies the reason why the short story has never been adequately defined.'
(H. E. Bates, *The Modern Short Story: Retrospect,* Michael Joseph, 1972)

'The American writer, Michael Chabon, editor of McSweeney's *Mammoth Treasury of Thrilling Tales*, pours scorn on the idea of the short story as "something glimpsed out of a window", or a personal crisis, revealed in a "moment of truth". He believes in telling stories. He admires Munro, who was never doing that kind of intense and simplified work. Her stories can contain as much life as most novels. Her plots can twist, and turn, and the tale can turn out to be about something quite different from what it set out to discuss. She can look at the same world through a microscope at one moment, and through a telescope the next, at a human being from inside and outside his or her mind, at an event as a decisive, tragic moment and simultaneously as a flat part of the inexorable process of time and ageing.'
AS Byatt on Alice Munro, 'Everything is Illuminated' Guardian Review, 04.03.06

Similarities and differences between novels and short stories

Both novels and short stories contain the same ingredients. They both have character(s), conflicts, themes and events. They both employ plots and settings. They both use narration, description and dialogue.

Most writers would agree that the main difference between a novel and a short story is its length. Novels are generally between 60,000 – 120,000 words. 30,000 - 60,000 words would qualify as a novella (or short novel) which means that anything less could be classified a short story. However, the majority of short stories are between 2,000 – 5,000 words (often because magazines and short story competitions specify such word limits but it is also a good length to practise).

There are other basic differences, but always remember there are exceptions!

Similarities and differences between novels and short stories

	Novels	Short stories
Setting (time & place)	Novels are able to cover vast expanses of time and space. They may span an entire lifetime of a character and/or several generations and include many locations.	Short stories need to be more constrained with time. They may only span a single day, or even a moment, and they are more limited in their locations.
Characters	Novels can host a larger cast of characters – although it is still important to focus on one character.	Short stories need to focus on one character. More than three characters is not advisable.
Event	There can be many events in a novel, and often big events.	There is usually a single (and often smaller) event in a short story.
Themes	There are often many themes within a novel (i.e. growing up, loss of innocence, dealing with death).	A short story usually reveals a single theme.
Plot	The plot can be more complex and may involve many sub-plots.	The plot may be nothing more than an event.
Conflict Internal (self against self) Personal (person against person) External (person against nature – wars, famines, earthquakes etc.)	There can be many areas of conflict (internal, personal and external).	Conflict is often singular and internal (should she take that new job or not… should she meet with a friend she hasn't seen for years or not…).

Comment on Robert Shuster's 'Eclipsed'

This very short story differs from Tillman's 'Little Tales' in that the event is singular and microscopic, capturing a moment in the boy's life. The time frame is linear and short and the story is told from the point of view of the little boy, Gavin. The narrative includes description, dialogue and internal narration - all seen through the boy's eyes. It has a beginning, middle and end as Gavin prepares for the Eclipse, watches it and wants it to be over. In that brief moment when the sun is blotted out the boy tries to imagine what it is like to grow old and to die. As Gavin takes off his eclipse viewer, all colours appear to be reversed. This use of imagery could be seen as an allusion to the passing of time.

Part 2

Aristotle

Aristotle was born more than 2000 years ago in 384 BC. He studied at Athens in the Academy of Plato. Sometime later he became the tutor of the young Alexander the Great. When Alexander succeeded to the throne of Macedonia in 335, Aristotle established his school and research Institute, the Lyceum in Athens. After Alexander's death in 323, anti-Macedonian caused Aristotle to flee to Chalcis in Euboea, where he died in 322.

During his life he lectured and wrote extensively on a number of subjects ranging from philosophy, physics, zoology, politics, rhetoric and poetics. These works, translated, shaped the development of mediaeval thought, first in the Arab world, then in the Latin West, where Aristotle came to be regarded as the source of all knowledge.

He is not quite so highly thought of in the 21st century but, in particular, *Poetics*, is still very influential. In retrospect, Aristotle could be regarded as the first structuralist. In contemporary terminology structuralism does for narrative what grammar does for language in that it provides rules to explain the structure of narrative, as grammar provides rules to explain the structure of language. Aristotle's analysis of narrative is as relevant today as it was during his lifetime. Even though he focuses on Greek tragedy, his observations could easily be applied to Hollywood. It is perhaps not surprising that many scriptwriters refer to Aristotle.

What we read today are not the books which Aristotle prepared - sadly, these did not survive - but his notes. These writings can be very obscure and open to interpretation. For example, there are still fundamental disagreements between 'harmatia' and 'katharsis'. Nevertheless, they are well worth having a look at.

The following extract is taken from *Poetics*, (Penguin, 1966, p13)

5. Plot: basic concepts

5.1 *Completeness*

We have laid down that tragedy is an imitation of a complete, i.e. whole, action, possessing a certain magnitude. (There is such a thing as a whole which possesses no magnitude.) A *whole* is that which has a beginning, a middle and an end. A *beginning* is that which itself does not follow necessarily from anything else, but some second thing naturally exists or occurs after it. Conversely, an *end* is that which does itself naturally follow from something else, either necessarily or in general, but there is nothing else after it. A *middle* is that which itself comes after something else, and some other thing comes after it. Well constructed plots should therefore not begin or end at any arbitrary point, but should employ the stated forms.

Types of conflict

There are generally accepted to be three types of conflict: person against person (personal), person against self (internal) and person against nature (external - natural and manmade disasters). In its purest form, theatre is particularly suited to personal conflict, prose to internal (as you are telling the story through a character) and film to external conflict (cf. Hollywood) but all genres tend to use all types of conflicts – sometimes all three in one scene/chapter.

Vladimir Propp

Vladimir Propp, a Russian folklorist, analysed the structure of Russian folktales and came up with a formula which governed all the tales. He claimed that there is a possibility of thirty-one functions and up to seven characters. Below is a simplified version of Propp's narrative rules adapted from *Morphology of the Folktale* (University of Texas Press, 1958 - first published in 1928)

Propp claims that the action of most tales develops within the limits of these functions. **Not every plot contains all the functions**, but the functions must necessarily occur in order.

THE FUNCTIONS OF DRAMATIS PERSONAE

Introduction or mention of hero.

1. Someone from the family leaves home.
2. A prohibition is addressed to the hero.
3. The prohibition is violated.
4. The villain makes an attempt at reconnaissance.
5. The villain receives information about his victim.
6. The villain attempts to deceive his victim in order to take possession of him or his belongings.
7. The victim is deceived and therefore unwittingly helps his enemy.
8. The villain harms a member of the family.
8a. Someone in the family either lacks something or desires to have something.
9. The misfortune or lack is made known. The hero is approached with a request or command. He is allowed to go or is dispatched somewhere.
10. The hero agrees to seek someone/something.
11. The hero leaves home.
12. The hero is tested/interrogated/attacked. This prepares the way for him to receive either a magical agent or helper.
13. The hero reacts to the actions of the future donor.
14. The hero acquires the use of a magical agent.
15. The hero is transferred, delivered, or led to the whereabouts of an object of search.
16. The hero and villain join in direct combat.
17. The hero is branded/wounded.
18. The villain is defeated.
19. The initial misfortune or lack is resolved.
20. The hero returns.
21. The hero is pursued.
22. The hero is rescued from pursuit.
23. The hero, unrecognised, arrives home or in another country.
24. A false hero presents unfounded claims.
25. A difficult task is proposed to the hero.
26. The task is resolved.
27. The hero is recognised.
28. The false hero or villain is exposed.
29. The hero is given a new appearance.
30. The villain is punished.
31. The hero is married and ascends the throne.

Seven character types

Characters are described as 'spheres of action' (p.79).

1. Villain
2. Donor
3. Helper
4. Princess (or sought for person)
5. Dispatcher
6. Hero
7. False hero

'In addition, there exist special personages for connections (complainers, informers, slanderers).'

Characterisation

There are many layers to a character. Characterisation generally refers to the external appearance of a character and therefore represents some of the outer layers. It is the little characteristics that make a character stand out. There are several things to focus on here. Firstly, the detail about the kind of clothes a character wears - maybe their trousers are always a little too big, or maybe they insist on wearing a hat? Secondly, their body language - maybe they walk in a particular manner, or prefer to be barefooted wherever possible, or hold a cigarette in a certain way? Maybe they constantly play with their hair, tap their fingers on a table or chew the tops of pens? Thirdly, little individual traits - maybe they insist on only drinking lemon tea, are vegetarian or refuse to go on aeroplanes. Fourthly, how do they speak? Perhaps they have a particular accent or their own catch phrase? Do they often shout?

When thinking of characteristics, there are two things to consider.

1. A character's background (is there something which has happened to the character in the past which has caused the character to behave/express themselves in a particular or curious way - consider both genetic and cultural influences?)

2. Their state of mind at the time of writing (if a character is nervous or agitated - consciously or unconsciously - it may be causing him or her to display nervous characteristics).

True character

We have already suggested that a compelling character is not always what he or she seems. What are his or her contradictions? What does the character want? Knowingly or unknowingly? Why does the character want what s/he wants? A character must always surprise the reader. Therefore, true character is revealed when the character has to make some kind of decision or react to a particular incident and this is where plot and character work together. True character represents the inner layers of a character. Is he or she really a strong or weak person? Selfish or kind? An impostor or genuine?

Sources for Characters

There are many ways in which you can come across characters. You may see someone who intrigues you and decide to develop an imaginary character from observation. You might know someone - or more than one person and combine their personalities/physiques. Portraits or photographs of people you don't know could be another way of developing a character by re-imagining their lives. Obituaries can also offer interesting perceptions into people's lives.

Studies of psychology and, in particular, personality types can also be useful. In particular enneagrams (based on nine different personality types) have become popular recently and there are numerous books on the subject. If you are interested, *The Enneagram Made Easy* by Renee Baron & Elizabeth Wagele, (Harper San Francisco, 1994) is useful. Horoscopes can also help define characterisation

Character Creation Form

Name	
Age	
Male/female	
Sexuality	
Address	
Description of house(s)	
Education/ work history	
Qualifications	
Profession	
Workplace	
Hobbies	
PHYSICAL APPEARANCE OF CHARACTER	
Height	
Eye colour	
Facial characteristics	
Physique	

TYPE OF CLOTHES WORN	
Home	
Work	
Social occasions	
HABITS/QUIRKS	
Physical	
Verbal	
PERSONALITY	
Attitudes (likes/ dislikes)	
Strengths	
Weaknesses	
Beliefs	
Religious/ political/ moral	

AUTOBIOGRAPHICAL DETAIL	
Parents	
Siblings	
Childhood memories/ traumas	
Special relationships	
True character	

Functions of dialogue

- breathes life into the characters and adds authenticity to the story
- conveys the thoughts and emotions of a character (cf. what he says, what he thinks he said and what he hides) - thereby creating conflict, tension and suspense
- moves the story forward
- can summarise past events without need for lengthy explanation
- sets a scene (as opposed to summary), providing a gear change in pacing (e.g. from slow description and/or narration)

Real dialogue is often full of hesitations (erm, yeah, you know, know what I mean....), unfinished sentences, changes in subject and the content is often boring. Therefore, reading 'real dialogue' can be tiresome. What you need to aim for is an *impression* of real speech.

Opening extract from *How late it was, how late*, James Kelman (Minerva, 1995)

Ye wake in a corner and stay there hoping yer body will disappear, the thoughts smothering ye; these thoughts; but ye want to remember and face up to things, just something keeps ye from doing it, why can ye no do it; the words filling yer head: then the other words; there's something wrong; there's something far far wrong; ye're no a good man, ye're just no a good man. Edging back into awareness, of where ye are: here, slumped in this corner, with these thoughts filling ye. And oh christ his back was sore; stiff, and the head pounding. He shivered and hunched up his shoulders, shut his eyes, rubbed into the corners with his fingertips; seeing all kinds of spots and lights. Where in the name of fuck...

He was here, he was leaning against auld rusty palings, with pointed spikes, some missing or broke off. And he looked again and saw it was a wee bed of grassy weeds, that was what he was sitting on. His feet were back in view. He studied them; he was wearing an auld pair of trainer shoes for fuck sake where had they come from he had never seen them afore man auld fucking trainer shoes. The laces werenay even tied! Where was his leathers? A new pair of leathers man he got them a fortnight ago and now here they were fucking missing man know what I'm saying, somebody must have blagged them, miserable bastards, what chance ye got. And then left him with these. Some fucking deal. Unless they thought he was dead; fair enough, ye could see that, some poor cunt scratching himself and thinking, Naybody's there, naybody's there; so why no just take them, the guy's dead, take them, better that than them just sitting there going to waste, disintegrating christ sake why no just take them. Fucking bastard he should have checked properly. Maybe he did; and saw he wasnay dead after all so he just exchanged them, stuck on the trainer shoes.

Comment on *How late it was, how late*

Kellman captures Sammy's Scottish voice by playing with word order, colloquialisms ('man know what I'm saying', 'what chance ye got') and he is consistent in his use of ye (you), yer (your), ye're (you're), nay (no), werenay (weren't), no (not) etc.

How to carry dialogue

Elmore Leonard writes that you should never use a verb other than 'said' to carry dialogue. This might be extreme but the problem with using other verbs such as 'intoned', 'emitted', 'buzzed', 'asserted', 'articulated', 'blurted', 'boomed', 'vocalised', 'iterated' etc. is that they draw attention to themselves and away from the characters and the dialogue. Sometimes though, verbs can help delineate the characters, as in Christopher Isherwood's use of 'drawled' and 'cooed' below.

An extract from Christopher Isherwood's 'Goodbye to Berlin' in *The Berlin Novels* (Vintage Classics, 1999, pp 267-269)

'I'm speaking a lousy English just now,' drawled Fritz, with great self-satisfaction. 'Sally says maybe she'll give me a few lessons.'

'Who's Sally?'

'Why, I forgot. You don't know Sally. Too bad of me. Eventually she's coming around here this afternoon.'

'Is she nice?'

Fritz rolled his naughty black eyes, handing me a rum-moistened cigarette from his patent tin:

'*Mar*-vellous!' he drawled. 'Eventually I believe I'm getting crazy about her.'

'And who is she? What does she do?'

'She's an English girl, an actress: sings at the Lady Windermere - hot stuff, believe me!'

'That doesn't sound much like an English girl, I must say.'

'Eventually she's got a bit of French in her. Her mother was French.'

A few minutes later, Sally herself arrived.

'Am I terribly late, Fritz darling?'

'Only half of an hour, I suppose,' Fritz drawled, beaming with proprietary pleasure. 'May I introduce Mr Isherwood - Miss Bowles? Mr Isherwood is commonly known as Chris.'

'I'm not,' I said. 'Fritz is about the only person who's ever called me Chris in my life.'

Sally laughed. She was dressed in black silk, with a small cape over her shoulders and a little cap like a page-boy's stuck jauntily on one side of her head:

'Do you mind if I use your telephone, sweet?'

'Sure. Go right ahead.' Fritz caught my eye. 'Come into the other room, Chris. I want to show you something.' He was evidently longing to hear my first impressions of Sally, his new acquisition.

'For heaven's sake, don't leave me alone with this man!' she exclaimed. 'Or he'll seduce me down the telephone. He's most terribly passionate.'

As she dialled the number, I noticed that her fingernails were painted emerald green, a colour unfortunately chosen, for it called attention to her hands, which were much stained by cigarette smoking and as dirty as a little girl's. She was dark enough to be Fritz's sister. Her face was long and thin, powdered dead white. She had very large brown eyes which should have been darker, to match her hair and the pencil she used for her eyebrows.

'Hilloo,' she cooed, pursing her brilliant cherry lips as though she was going to kiss the mouthpiece: 'Ist das Du, mein Liebling?' Her mouth opened in a fatuously sweet smile. Fritz and I sat watching her, like a performance at the theatre. 'Was wollen wir machen, Morgen Abend? Oh wie wunderbar... Nein, nein, ich werde bleiben Heute Abend zu Hause. Ja, ja, ich werde wirklich bleiben zu Hause... Auf Wiedersehen, mein Liebling...'

She hung up the receiver and turned to us triumphantly.

'That's the man I slept with last night,' she announced.

Forms of narration

Person	Authorial Stance/Mode
First **I**	**First person narrative:** **(storyteller, intrusive narrator, reliable narrator/ unreliable narrator, letter/diary forms, skaz)**
Second **YOU**	**Second person narrative**
Third **HE/SHE**	**Omniscient narrative** **Third person restricted narrative:** • Intimate 3rd person (subjective – internal POV) • Detached 3rd person (objective – external POV) • Multiple viewpoint (subjective - internal POV) • Multiple viewpoint (objective - external POV)

Comment on *Eclipse of the Sun* and *Sense and Sensibility*

Jane Austen's omniscient narrative moves from character to character as well as giving an overview as to what is happening in the Dashwood family, whereas *Eclipse of the Sun* presents a restricted third person narrative. The novel is divided between the two different narrative voices, Sumila and Rajesh. Each character tells their part of the story in their voice. This is what we mean when we say that you must tell a story *through* a character rather than about a character. Here each narrative is divided by an asterisk.

Third person narratives

Student example of detached, intimate and omniscient (by Patrick Barrett)

Detached 3rd Person

Paul had taken Karen punting in Stratford. The river's surface was smooth but a passing coal barge on a steady course caused such rough waves that Paul dropped the pole.

'I'd better dive in and get it out,' he said. 'It's a hot day, so I should dry off quickly,' he added with a fleeting thumbs-up gesture. Karen remained silent, her face slightly pale.

Karen eventually nodded. Within less than two minutes, Paul was back in the punt, a broad smile breaking out across his face as he dried off in the afternoon sunshine. Karen said nothing.

Intimate 3rd Person

Paul had taken Karen punting in Stratford, hoping to win her over with this display of romance - although she struck Paul as unusually quiet today. The river's surface was smooth, but Paul's heart sank as he saw a coal barge coming the other way. Please don't let me screw up on our first proper date, he thought as the monstrous vessel approached. But the barge caused such rough waves - was it deliberate, he wondered - that Paul knew it was either him or the pole, so he let go of the pole.

'I'd better dive in and get it out,' he said, hoping that Karen would admire his decisiveness. But she just sat there, silent and slightly pale. 'It's a hot day, so I should dry off quickly,' he added with feigned confidence, the irony of it just beginning to register with him.

Thankfully Paul was sure he had made a good impression as he watched Karen eventually nod. Within less than two minutes - although it felt like two hours - Paul was back in the punt, proud of his effort and enjoying the comforting warmth of the afternoon sunshine as it dried him off. 'I wonder why she is still so quiet though,' he asked himself.

Omniscient Narrative

Paul had taken Karen punting in Stratford, hoping to win her over with this display of romance - not realising that Karen didn't care for boats. The river's surface was smooth, but Paul's heart sank as he saw a coal barge coming the other way. Please don't let me screw up on our first proper date, he thought, as the monstrous vessel approached. But the barge's skipper disliked punts because they got in the way of hard-working people trying to earn a living in this overpriced country. So, without even touching the throttles, he cynically chose a course which best suited him, and him alone, causing such rough waves that Paul knew it was either him or the pole, so he let go of the pole.

'I'd better dive in and get it out,' he said, hoping that Karen would admire his decisiveness. But she was too nervous to care and just wanted to get back to the riverbank as quickly as possible. 'It's a hot day, so I should dry off quickly,' he added with feigned confidence, the irony of it just beginning to register with him.

Mistakenly, Paul was sure he had made a good impression as he watched Karen eventually nod. If only the poor lad knew! Within less than two minutes - although it felt like two hours - Paul was back in the punt, proud of his effort and obviously enjoying the comforting warmth of the afternoon sunshine as it dried him off. Karen, however, thought she was going to be sick.

Part 3

Angela Carter and Raymond Carver

Extract from Angela Carter's 'The Company of Wolves', *The Bloody Chamber*, **Penguin Books, 1981**

Snow half-caked the lattice and she opened it to look into the garden. It was a white night of moon and snow; the blizzard whirled round the gaunt, grey beasts who squatted on their haunches among the rows of winter cabbage, pointing their sharp snouts to the moon and howling as if their hearts would break. Ten wolves; twenty wolves – so many wolves she could not count them, howling in concert as if demented or deranged. Their eyes reflected the light from the kitchen and shone like a hundred candles.

(Extract from Raymond Carver's 'Nobody Said Anything', *Where I'm Calling From*, **Harvill, 1993)**

I could hear them out in the kitchen. I couldn't hear what they were saying, but they were arguing. Then it got quiet and she started to cry. I elbowed George. I thought he would wake up and say something to them so they would feel guilty and stop. But George is such an asshole. He started kicking and hollering.

"Stop gouging me, you bastard," he said. "I'm going to tell!"

"You dumb chickenshit," I said. "Can't you wise up for once? They're fighting and Mom's crying. Listen!"

Student examples of 'Fiona'

Fiona shoved her ice cream at him, threw her scarf around her neck and stormed out of the restaurant. As the icy blast of January hit her, she wished she had collected her coat; but she would not go back. She stamped her feet as she waited for the bus. Even that irregular metal vehicle offered more warmth, reliability and human contact than the empty frame she had left with her cold dessert. Selfish, hypocritical, heartless bastard. If that was him hooting his horn across the road, he could just drop dead.

A woman's head appeared from the little Fiat. 'Wanna lift? You OK? Whereya going?' It was that nosey bloody waitress who was supposed to be her friend.

'I'm just waiting for someone,' she lied through gritted teeth. 'You go on ahead.'

When she arrived home, soaked and shivering, she almost wished she had accepted the lift. But she had needed to be alone. Even the torrential rain had failed to quell her anger with her soon-to-be ex-fiancé. (Robert Perks)

Bus number 968 flashed on the slim digital screen like an ominous word or a code. Absinth or SOS. Numbers are no different than words.
    'I hate asparagus,' he had said in the restaurant. 'In fact, I hate you too.'
    Inside the thick impenetrable structure that was the bus stop, adverts for sanitary towels, eye shadows and bank loans rolled one after the other in slow motion. The wind blew pieces of paper in the air. A yellow plastic bag whirled about making soft rustling sounds.
    I didn't pay, she thought. And I didn't say goodbye.
    The highway was almost empty. The persistent horn from across the road sounded pointless and annoying like an alarm set off by accident.
    A woman shouted behind the half open window. "Hello, there. Want a lift?"
    She motioned with her hand. No.
    'Global warming,' he had said. 'That's the reason behind the shit weather.'
    Far into the distance the sun cut through the clouds like a laser beam.
    I'll wait for the sunshine and then I'll go back. Any minute now the rain will stop, she thought. (Evangelia Avloniti)

Metaphors and Similes

Similes from Raymond Chandler's *Farewell, my lovely* (Penguin, 1940)

Even on Central Avenue, not the quietest dressed street in the world, he looked about as inconspicuous as a tarantula on a slice of angel food. (p7)

There was a sudden silence as heavy as a waterlogged boat. (p10)

The barman goggled and his Adam's apple flopped around like a headless chicken. (p13)

The hunch I had was as vague as the heat waves that danced above the sidewalk. (p21)

His smile was as cunning as a broken mousetrap. (*ibid*)

Metaphors from *My Summer of Love* by Helen Cross (Bloomsbury, 2001)

I tutted and turned away, me hormones were rioting, setting light to cars and uprooting trees. (p12)

Dad met him once and said: *That bloke'd be out of his depth in a towpath puddle...* (p19)

I could see a dark drool of lace dribbling from the drawer where I'd drunkenly stuffed the underwear. (p29)

It was so rich and characterful a house; the ivy, the walled gardens, the stone lion/dog, those high thick doors, that it got gossiped about like a person. (p43)

If the Fakenham House was a person it would be an ancient alcoholic actress from the era of silent films, with an ashy cigarette in an ivory holder and a crude circle of rouge over papery cheeks. (p64)

I let the sentence float and settle in the junk-room part of my mind where I now heaped all unsettling phrases, thoughts and emotions. (p144)

Revise your own work (suggested criteria for fiction)

Research, setting and description
Is the setting/period sufficiently researched to be convincing? Is there enough telling detail to make the world believable without being overly descriptive? Or is there too much reliance on generalisation? Can the reader experience the atmosphere and the location with the characters?

Structure
Is the story arc fully realised? Is there a beginning, a middle and an end - not necessarily in that order? Is there an epiphany, a moment of truth for the character? Is the narrative controlled? Are the events surprising? Is there an overall sense of clarity? Is the progression of characters and events logical, or is the whole story too confusing? Does the opening hook the reader? Does the first paragraph establish the main character, set the scene and/or hint at the conflict to come? Is the story within a specific time frame? Is the ending satisfying (not flat or cheating - 'it was all a dream')? Are all the episodes relevant to the story? Does the story avoid coincidence? Is the back story released subtly throughout? Is it appropriately paced? Is there a clear theme?

Character
Is the right character telling the story? Does the character have a distinct voice? Are the characters fully rounded? Is there sufficient conflict (internal, personal, extra-personal) and tension between the characters/events? Are the motives of the characters understandable and logical to the story? Is the story told *through* the character rather than about the character? Are the characters shown in action? Are all the characters necessary for the story?

Dialogue
Does the dialogue move the story forward? Does it capture the voice of the character(s)? Are they distinct voices – does the dialogue capture the rhythms of speech? Is it an authentic impression of real speech? Does it create tension, conflict, suspense? Does it contrast the thoughts and emotions of the character? Does it provide a gear change in pacing? Is it clear who is speaking?

Point of view
Is the point of view consistent throughout? Are there careless shifts in psychic distance (i.e. from detached 3rd person to intimate 3rd person)? Is it an effective way of telling the story?

Writing
Is there variation in pacing? Is there an appropriate balance between description, action and dialogue? Is there sufficient showing, not telling? Is

the writing succinct? Is the writing fresh and original? Or is the writing full of clichés? Are there any unnecessary adjectives/adverbs? Does the writing avoid abstract words/images? Is there inappropriate or excessive use of the passive voice? Are there shifts in diction level? Are there faulty rhythms or accidental rhymes? Does the writing overstate/understate a particular scene? Has the writing been spell/grammar checked? Is the writing correctly punctuated?

Originality, sophistication and depth of understanding
Is the story an original idea or an original angle to an idea? Is it imaginative and sophisticated in its approach? Does it demonstrate a deep understanding of writing?

Presentation
Is the work carefully presented? Is the dialogue set out in an acceptable publishing format? Does the story follow the general rules for publishing?

Hooking the reader

As we can see from the extracts, there is no one way of hooking a reader: different readers respond differently. However, there are certain things that a beginning should do. These include:

- introduce main character
- hint at conflict/quest and or problem faced by main character
- set the scene
- establish mood/tone
- establish narrative voice

Openings

Orwell's well-known opening of *1984* immediately sets the then futuristic scene with the clocks striking thirteen and the glass doors of Victory Mansions. It also settles the reader into a third person narrative: 'It was a...'. The mood is established by the vile wind and gritty dust. The main character, Winston Smith, is introduced in the second sentence. Even without knowing his age, the fact that he is trying to escape the wind and 'not quickly enough' implies that he is not a young man. The scene is further enhanced in the next paragraph by smells of the hallway, the lift that doesn't work, the mention of Hate Week and the poster of the enormous face which underlines the conflict and, more precisely, the antagonist.

Likewise, in **Tracy Chevalier's** *Girl With a Pearl Earring*, the main character is immediately introduced through the first person narrative and much about her and her relationship with her mother and the society she lives in is revealed by her surprise that her mother did not tell her 'they' were coming. It is also established that the narrator is narrating from a later point in her life, which allows her a certain amount of retrospection. The conflict is clear in that first sentence and, as she did not cry, the narrative hints that what happens next is unexpected. The scene is established, again through the senses, the sounds of the voices and we are told of the year. The atmosphere of the setting is enforced by the similes, 'bright as polished brass' and 'low and dark like the table'. The fact that she can hear 'rich carpets' in their voices tells us that they from a wealthier social background than she is. The narrative hook is cast: who are 'they' and what happens to this young girl?

In **Yann Martel's** *Life of Pi*, another first person narrative, again the main character is introduced in the first sentence. We are told that he has suffered which immediately shifts the narrative into gear as we want to know what has happened to him. The narrator's setting at the time of writing, we are told, is Toronto and the tale he is about to tell pre-dates this time. The details of his strange religious practices and unusual studies are intriguing, particularly his chosen zoology thesis on the functional analysis of the thyroid gland of the three-toed sloth. This strange choice gives us a taste of the narrative tone which, while entertaining and often playful, narrates the bizarre and extreme tale of survival.

In all the above openings, the main character, the setting, the narrative voice, tone and conflict are either introduced or hinted at. Likewise, you should introduce your main character immediately, avoiding long descriptions and explanations. There is probably something wrong with your story if by the end of the second page you haven't introduced the above. It is no use having a fantastic scene on page five - the reader may not get that far. Begin, instead, on page five.

Opening lines of books

i) *Harry Potter and the Philosopher's Stone* J.K.Rowling (Bloomsbury,1997)
ii) *Catch-22*, Joseph Heller (first published 1961)
iii) *Hard Times*, Charles Dickens (first published in 1854)
iv) *Kane and Abel*, Geoffrey Archer (first published in 1979)
v) *Jane Eyre*, Charlotte Bronte (first published in 1847)
vi) *The Day of the Jackal*, Frederick Forsyth (first published in 1971)
vii) *Unnatural Causes,* P.D. James (first published in 1976)
viii) *The Sea*, John Banville (Picador, 2005)

Authors' Note & Acknowledgments

Many many thanks to the following authors, agents and publishers who have granted permission to use copyright material gratis:

The Girl with a Pearl Earring reprinted with permission of HarperCollins Publishers Ltd © Tracy Chevalier, 1999.
Bridget Jones' Diary © Helen Fielding, 1996.
The Berlin Novels © Christopher Isherwood, 1935.
Poetics by Aristotle, translated by Malcolm Heath (Penguin Classics, 1996) © Malcolm Heath, 1996.
Eclipse of the Sun by Phil Whitaker, 1997, Phoenix House (division of The Orion Publishing Group).
Lolita by Vladimir Nabokov, Weidenfeld & Nicholson (division of The Orion Publishing Group).
Collected Stories of Graham Greene by Graham Greene, Penguin, 1986.
My Summer of Love © Helen Cross, 2001.
1984 by George Orwell (Copyright © George Orwell, 1949) by permission of Bill Hamilton as the Literary Executor of the Estate of the Late Sonia Brownell Orwell and Secker & Warburg Ltd. and the publishers Harcourt Brace.
How Late It Was, How Late by James Kelman, published by Secker & Warburg. Reprinted by permission of The Random House Group Ltd.
Grace © Carrie Worrall, 1998.
'Little Tales of New York' published in *The Time Out Book of New York Short Stories*, ed Nicholas Royle (Penguin, 1997) © Lynne Tillman, 1997.

Every effort has been made to reach copyright holders. The authors would like to hear from anyone whose rights they have unknowingly infringed.